DIARY OF A DISCIPLE:
PETER & PAUL'S STORY

Gemma Willis

Illustrated by Emma Randall

Copyright © Scripture Union 2017
First published 2017

ISBN 978 1 78506 569 9

The right of Gemma Willis to be identified as author of this work has been asserted by her in accordance with the Copyright, Designs and Patents Act 1988.

Emma Randall has asserted her right under the Copyright, Designs and Patents Act 1988, to be identified as illustrator of this work.

British Library Cataloguing-in-Publication Data. A catalogue record of this book is available from the British Library.

Printed in India by Thomson Press India Ltd

Cover and internal design by Emma Randall

Scripture Union is an international Christian charity working with churches in more than 130 countries.

Thank you for purchasing this book. Any profits from this book support SU in England and Wales to bring the good news of Jesus Christ to children, young people and families and to enable them to meet God through the Bible and prayer.

Find out more about our work and how you can get involved at:
www.scriptureunion.org.uk (England and Wales)
www.suscotland.org.uk (Scotland)
www.suni.co.uk (Northern Ireland)
www.scriptureunion.org (USA)
www.su.org.au (Australia)

CHAPTER 1

IT JUST GETS BETTER

Well, **hello** there. How very **WONDERFUL** to

see you, my friend. I don't know if we've met before, but

in a way that doesn't matter because I'm meeting you **NOW**!

Allow me to introduce myself — my name is **Luke**. I'm

an (average) sort of guy, with (average) sort of hair

and (average) sort of eyes, except I feel a bit like

my eyes have been out on stalks these past few years,

because I've seen so many **AMAZING**, incredible

totally mind-boggling **THINGS**.

Sorry — I'm getting carried away already. I meant to

say, I'm a **doctor**, you know, the kind that makes people

better when they're ill... But I don't want to (tell) you

about FIXING snotty noses, mending broken elbows

ouch!

and clipping rotten toe nails. NO. I want to tell you

a story that gets better and better and **BETTER**

and BETTER and even more **BETTERER** still!

OK, so there are a few things you *NEED* to know.

12 things, in fact:

1 There was this guy called **JESUS**. He was pretty epic.

2 He was born in a barn, in Bethlehem, with some
cows and sheep, and all their smells.

3 His mum was called **MARY**, and his dad was Joseph.

Well, sort of — Joseph was his dad, but so was **GOD**

too (complicated — *I KNOW!*).

3

4 Angels had told **MARY** that she was going to have a super **SPECIAL** baby.

5 And the angels were right. Jesus _was_ **SUPER** special.

6 When Jesus grew up he did some truly "awesome" stuff. He made **sick** people well, he walked on water, he fed **THOUSANDS** of people with two fish and five loaves of bread, and soooo much more. Jesus chose 12 lads to follow him. IN FACT, **LOADS** of people followed Jesus everywhere!

If you want to find out a bit more about all the awesome stuff that Jesus did then grab a Bible and find a bit in it called "The Gospel of Luke" or, if you like, you can also find it here: www.diaryofadisciple.org.

7 So Jesus, **GOD'S** Son, did all these **AMAZING** things, but he <u>only</u> did them because he wanted people to realise how wonderful God is and how much he (loves) them. He wanted everyone to know that God was giving them a **chance** to love him back.

8 But even though Jesus did **GREAT** things, and he was God's <u>Son</u>, not **everyone** liked him very much. [IN FACT], some people hated him — so much, that they made a plan to **KILL** him. Nasty.

9 And they **DID**. One day, when Jesus and his mates were having a special meal together, he <u>suddenly</u> started saying that *SOMEONE* in the room was going to hand him over to the bad guys. And then <u>everything</u> happened so fast.

10 The BAD guys got him. They nailed him to a cross outside Jerusalem. They killed him even though he'd done nothing wrong. That was the worst day EVER. It was like everything had stopped.

11 But it hadn't. Because three days later, he was back! Mind-boggling, right? He was **DEAD**. Definitely **TOTALLY DEAD**, inside a big tomb, with an enormous rock in the way, and then he wasn't there any more! He was alive!! Loads of people saw him: he walked, talked and ate fish.

12 Jesus hung around for a whole 40 days. And he had even more **AMAZING** things to say to his mates. He told them they had to stay in Jerusalem and he promised that he'd send "the Holy Spirit" to help them. (I'll explain about that in a bit.) Then he disappeared. He was carried up to heaven by a cloud. Honestly — he was! And when he went up, two scary glowing angel men came down.

They asked Jesus' mates **why** ?? ?? they were staring at the sky (I mean, I know I would've been staring with my mouth open like a fish), and then they said: "You've just seen **JESUS** go to heaven, but he'll come **BACK** again, too, just like he went."

And **THAT**, my friends, is where we start this story.

SO. When the disciples (that's the posh name for Jesus' mates) had managed to close their fish mouths they walked back to **J**erusalem and went back to the **ROOM** where they'd been hanging out.

Peter, John, James, Andrew, Philip, Thomas, Bartholomew, Matthew,

another **James**, **Simon** and **Judas** just wanted to (talk) to God about **everything** that had happened. IN FACT, that's *pretty much* all they did. They prayed and prayed and prayed, and then prayed some MORE. **MARY** and her boys (Jesus' mum and brothers) joined in too, as well as a few OTHER women.

Peter was kind of in charge, and when everyone got together (there were about **120** people by now) he'd get up and do a LITTLE speech.

1, 2, 3 ...

If you can count, you **might've** noticed I said there were **12** of Jesus' mates whom he chose to follow him — and in that list I just wrote down there were only **11**.

9

I missed someone. **Judas**. (Not the one in the list, another one.) Judas was the one who let Jesus down. **HE** was the one who told the **bad** guys where they could find Jesus, all because they gave him a bag of silver.

Peter (told) **everyone** that Judas had bought a field with his bag of silver, but that when he'd gone to see it, he had a rather **HORRIBLE**, super **gory**, mightily messy accident and **DIED**. Eww. It was **SOOOO** gross and **GOOEY** that **everyone** who lived near the field called it "The field of blood". **BLEURGH.**

BUT, even though that was all a bit **GRIM**, Peter told everyone that God **KNEW** it was going to happen,

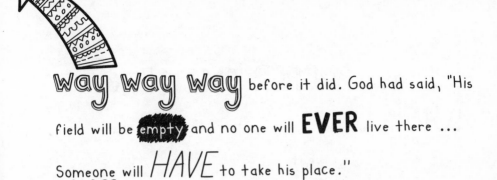

way way way before it did. God had said, "His field will be ~~empty~~ and no one will **EVER** live there ... Someone will *HAVE* to take his place."

And so that's what happened. Peter said someone who'd followed Jesus from the beginning, someone who'd seen it ALL and knew the story so far, would have to take Judas' place. So the disciples said it would have to be either Barsabbas or Matthias. But they didn't want to choose — they wanted GOD to do the choosing. hmmm

So, they asked God to SHOW them who it should be. And he did. Matthias became the new number 12.

Now it all gets PROPER EXCITING. I can't WAIT to tell you

what

happened

next!

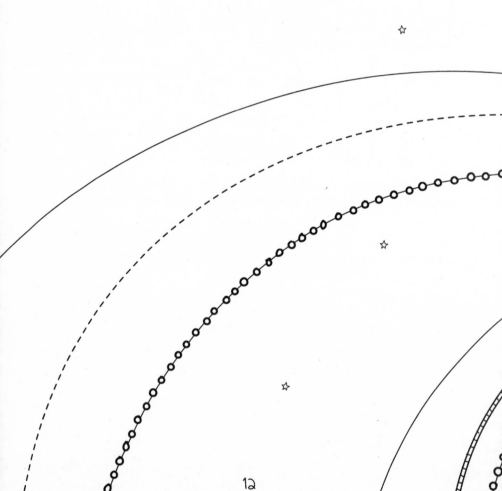

CHAPTER 2

WIND, WORDS & WONDER

Are you **ready**?! What happened next, totally
BLEW my **MIND**...

Imagine the sound of the loudest, most incredible, slightly
scary, strongest ever wind *blowing around*
a room. Are you imagining it? Well, that's what happened
to **JESUS'** followers when they were all together
enjoying their Pentecost **Party**.

DID YOU KNOW:

Jewish ✡ people gathered together to **celebrate**
Pentecost **every** year. Except they didn't actually
call it Pentecost, they called it *SHAVUOT*. But
either way, I **GUESS** you might be wondering
what on earth they were celebrating. Well, way back

14

when **Moses** was alive, God used to speak to him, and one day he gave Moses a **GREAT BIG** list of instructions that showed how people could live in the **BEST** way. If you have a Bible, you can find out all about it in the book of *Exodus.*

But it didn't just get a bit breezy, it was like an enormous whirlwind came from nowhere and filled up every single room. And **then** there were things like flames **everywhere,** but they didn't **burn** anyone or anything, they sat on top of everyone's heads. All at once, Jesus' followers started speaking in **DIFFERENT** languages — imagine what that must've sounded like!

Namaste

Bonjour

Hola

Whirlwinds, unburning FIRE, words no one had ever

heard before? Woah — that all sounds kind of "scary"

to me! The Holy Spirit had arrived with some serious style!

DID YOU KNOW:

the Holy Spirit appears in lots of DIFFERENT

ways in the Bible? Sometimes he's like a dove,

sometimes like fire, sometimes like wind, sometimes

like a VOICE, sometimes like a feeling... The Holy Spirit

isn't anything to be scared of, though, he's God, just like

Jesus is TOO. I know that seems pretty crazy,

how can GOD be Father, Son and Holy

Spirit all at once? I don't REALLY know how

he does it, but I know he does and he is AMAZING!

Outside there were **loads** and **loads** of people with **loads** and **loads** of wide-open mouths and thousands of staring eyes, and they were all **STARING** at Jesus' *followers*. They'd heard (all) the noise

WHERE DID ALL THAT WIND COME FROM?

DID YOU HEAR THAT NOISE?

HOW DO THEY KNOW ALL THOSE LANGUAGES?

WHAT ARE THEY SAYING?

and wanted to know what was going on. The weirdest thing was that even though some of the people in the **CROWDS** had come from countries hundreds of miles away to join in with the Pentecost **PARTY**, everyone could hear one of Jesus' followers talking in their **OWN** language. **HOW** were they speaking perfectly in a language they'd **NEVER** even heard before? All these **JESUS** people were from **G**alilee — they definitely didn't learn

17

a hundred **DIFFERENT** ᴘᴘ languages there! There were

people from ←all over→ the place, hearing all about

God's **AMAZING** ⟩power⟨ and the ``incredible'' things

he'd done — but they were hearing it in a language *THEY*

could understand.

But some people in the crowd just **LAUGHED**. ha ha ha The

[only] way they could *EXPLAIN* what was going on

was to say that the Jesus' followers had obviously had a bit

too much wine 🍷 🍾 at their Party, and were rather

embarrassingly drunk! But Peter knew they weren't drunk at all.
oooo

"What you're seeing and hearing didn't come from

drinking too much wine! It's just like God said

18

it would be: he told you that a day would come when he'd pour out his Spirit on everyone. It's the Spirit that makes people SEE what God shows them — young and old, men and women, rich and poor, they'll see glimpses of God's plan. When people hear GOD, they'll tell others what he says, and there'll be signs, too. Fire, blood, smoke and fog, the sun will go black and the moon will go red, and when all of these things HAPPEN, then Jesus will come back again, and when he does, everyone who has already asked him WILL be saved."

By now, everyone was listening to Peter. He didn't seem DRUNK — he was awake, alive, he was excited and he was talking like he had really important things to say.

He was almost jumping UP and DOWN. "Jesus was who he said he was. That man whom you killed, that INNOCENT man, GOD sent him to you, he really WAS God's Son, and he still IS. He showed you how INCREDIBLE God is — you saw Jesus do what you couldn't even imagine. I mean, he even came back to life!

"3 days after you killed † him, he was completely ALIVE again, a real person, a real living, talking man who EVEN cooked me breakfast on the beach. It was the BEST breakfast EVER! Death can't beat God, he's too powerful! It's just like KING David said so long ago:

I saw the Lord, he was always there, he was always

with me and he was AMAZING, he gave me HOPE and showed me *life* to the FULL. He will make me happy when I am with him.

"And I'm telling you," Peter carried on (and by now he really WAS jumping up and down), "David was absolutely right. He knew that God was going to do INCREDIBLE things. He knew, because God had TOLD him so, that someone from his family, WAY in the future, would be a NEW and DIFFERENT kind of king. That was King Jesus. And David knew that even death wouldn't be the end of Jesus. God told him that, too. All of us stood here, we're the ones who saw it all happen, everything God said he WOULD do, he HAS done. And all of you, standing there open-mouthed, it's all for YOU!

God [sent➜] Jesus, the man you killed. God sent his ONLY
Son and made him KING, a king sent to save us ALL!"

The CROWDS were pretty silent now. Peter was

so very, very EXCITED. Not only was he

jumping up and down as he spoke — but he waved his arms

around and his smile seemed to keep on getting wider

and wider! There were TEARS in the eyes of SO

MANY faces watching.

Slowly, but [surely,] you could see, they BEGAN

to realise what they'd done, who Jesus was and what it

all MEANT. They STARTED to ask what they could

do, as the tears rolled down their faces.

"It's NOT too late," said Peter. "ALL you have to

do is come back to God — come to Jesus. Be baptised and

know that everything you've done wrong will be forgiven.

"And when you're baptised, it won't JUST be with

water, it will be with the Holy Spirit too! God wants to save

everyone — you, your children, your children's children,

EVERY SINGLE PERSON he has made."

About 3,000 people from the CROWDS

were baptised, and the Holy Spirit did AMAZING

things in their lives, too. Peter and the others taught the

new believers everything they knew about Jesus,

and helped them to learn how to pray.

More and more mind-blowing things just kept on happening. Just as Jesus had PROMISED when he left his disciples on earth, the Holy Spirit really HAD come to HELP them and make incredible things happen.

All the people who believed in Jesus stayed together, and they shared everything they had — that way, everyone always had just what they needed. I mean, imagine sharing absolutely everything!? But they were genuinely happy, and constantly told God how wonderful he is — they couldn't thank him ENOUGH. Every day, more and more and more people came to join them... Wow, WOW, WOW! I told you it was AWESOME!

CHAPTER 3

MATS, MONEY & MIRACLES

A few days later, Peter and John were on their way to the TEMPLE when they saw a man who couldn't walk being carried inside on a mat.

It turned out that this man had NEVER been able to walk because his legs didn't WORK properly. Every day he was carried into the Temple and left in places where he could just SIT and BEG for money.

DID YOU KNOW:

The man HAD to beg for money, otherwise he wouldn't be able to buy Food or clothes, and no one would think of helping him. People left him at the Temple gates, where everyone walked past and maybe, just maybe, gave him a coin or two.

He saw **Peter** and **John** coming through the gate and he asked *THEM* for money, the same as **everyone** else, but Peter and John bent **DOWN** and looked into the man's eyes and said, Look at us. So he **DID**. He was *pretty* sure they were going to make a (big) donation — they wanted him to look them in the eyes so they could see if he was GRATEFUL or NOT. Right? But then Peter said: "I don't have **ANY** money for you, but I **CAN** give you something else, something *BETTER*. I give you what II have — in the name of JESUS CHRIST, get up and walk!"

What do you think happened **NEXT**?

a) The man *laughed* in their faces ☐

b) John said, "Peter, WHAT are you doing?" ☐

c) They all held hands ☐

d) Peter snee z e d ☐

e) The man stood UP and walked ☐

Keep reading to find out!

Peter held hands with the man, who jumped up as if he was a professional jumper — his legs were all " SPRINGY and NEW. He couldn't *believe* what had happened. He RAN into the TEMPLE, Peter and John behind him, shouting and saying thank you to GOD for healing him. Everyone in the Temple recognised him, after all they'd been walking PAST him and throwing money at him every day for YEARS,

but he was WALKING! On his own two le

WOOOOOOOOAH!

The man kept jumping and spinning around, waving

in the air and DANCING. He kept grabbing

and John and waving their arms, TOO, and people s

to form a crowd. They kept staring at the man, and tr

to reach in and poke his legs — they wanted to SEE wh

had happened; they wanted to know how he had been heale

"WHY are you all wondering what has happened?"

said Peter. "God is at work. It's JESUS. The

SAME Jesus that you all got rid of, the man you killed

when he was the ONE who came to bring life!

It was GOD who brought him ←back from the dead and we ALL saw him for ourselves. And faith in Jesus' power made this man walk— it's believing in Jesus that has made him strong for you all to SEE!"

John could see every KIND of expression looking back at Peter. There were happy faces, sad faces, ANGRY faces, peaceful faces, CONFuSEd faces, scared faces and so many others...

"It was only through what you DID to Jesus that God's plan happened as he'd said it would all along. God made it all work out, so turn back to him, say you're sorry, start over, let God make you NEW

and then he'll send Jesus ◁back. He'll come back from heaven, and then everything will be made *PERFECT.*

That's what God has been saying through his messengers since the start of TIME. Through Moses he told people that he would send Jesus, and that **everyone** needed to listen to what he said. Through Samuel he said it **again**, and through all of the OTHER messengers he sent, he *KEPT ON* telling us what he was going to do. He kept on calling us back to him. And he **KEPT** his promise. When he promised Abraham that through his future FAMILY there would be good things for ALL people, he meant it. And that's you, YOU are that future family; Abraham was your great great great great (as many greats as you can imagine) GRANDAD!

God *longs* to give you **GOOD** things, and that's **WHY** he sent Jesus, to make everything right again!"

SERIOUSLY — this was all so, so, so awesome! You'd 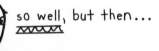everyone would've been *pretty* STUNNED by what Peter said, **everything** seemed to be going so well, but then...

CHAPTER 4

GRUMPS, GRABBING & GROUND SHAKERS

... things didn't go so well.

Some grumpy religious leaders in the TEMPLE had been watching Peter and John. They were pretty peeved that people were LISTENING to all this Jesus (talk.) Peter and John had NO RIGHT to come here and tell people that Jesus had come back from the dead; they were whipping up the crowds and getting them all EXCITED. As far as they were concerned, that was absolutely not OK.

They grabbed Peter and John and yanked them away from the CROWDS. And then they arrested them and locked them up. They thought a night in jail might help **everyone** to forget about these two *losers*.

Only, their plan didn't _quite_ work. When people **HEARD**
what Peter and John had been saying and saw the
AMAZING things that happened, **5,000**
of them decided to become *believers*.

In the **morning**, the **grumpy** religious leaders
got together with all their **grumpy** religious friends
and *DRAGGED* Peter and John out of jail. They
made them stand up in front of **everyone** and then
asked them like a **MILLION?** questions. (Well, maybe
not **QUITE** that many — but I'm **SURE** it
must've seemed like that!)

> What makes you think you have the _right_ to do this?

> Where do you say your power comes from?

NOW, I don't know about **YOU**, but I'd have been pretty **scared**. I mean, these people had the {power} to make pretty **BAD** things happen — they'd killed Jesus after all. But Peter was as cool as a cucumber, because the Holy Spirit was there **with** him, giving him words to say.

? ? ? ?

"OK. If you're asking us questions because something **GOOD** happened, because a man who couldn't walk is now running around, then **let** me tell you, it's Jesus who **HEALED** him! The same Jesus whom you put on a cross and left to **DIE**. The same Jesus whom God made alive again! **This** Jesus, the one whom you REJECTED, he's the one who's holding **everything** together. No one else can save you, it's ONLY Jesus."

The TEMPLE leaders stared at Peter and John. I think they'd quite like to have PUNCHED them both on the nose ⇩ because they didn't seem able to stop talking about this JESUS.

And then it dawned on them. Peter and John looked rather familiar. Where had they been seen before?

THAT'S IT. They were two of those who'd been with Jesus before he died.

It's not **even like** they'd learned all this stuff by studying properly, they'd just followed ⟹ **JESUS** around, and now they were healing people and saying it was **ALL** Jesus. I mean, that man with the **dodgy** legs, he was *STILL* running around all over the place, and he was **DEFINITELY** the guy who hadn't been able to walk — no debate about that. Peter and John had answered **every** question they were asked, so the **grumpy** leaders told them to go and wait outside.

"What are we going to **DO?** How can we get **RID** of them?" they said. "Everyone knows what happened, **LOADS** of people saw it for themselves, and then they've told everyone **they** know. Let's tell Peter and John that they're [not allowed] to mention Jesus, not allowed to (talk) about him **ever** again." They were convinced that would **FIX** everything. Great plan — **right**? When the Temple leaders *TOLD* Peter and John that they weren't allowed to mention Jesus ever again, **WELL**, what do **YOU** think they said?

☐ Oh OK. **Sorry**, we'll not mention him **again**.

☐ Can we talk about Jesus if we just call him Robert instead?

☐ We can't (stop) talking about Jesus, and everything he did and said. He's too **AWESOME!**

Peter and John told them it was impossible to stop talking about Jesus: he'd changed their *lives*, he'd done amazing things, they couldn't just pretend it had **NEVER** happened.

They knew that God WANTED them to tell everyone about Jesus — it didn't matter if the Temple leaders weren't so keen... so they just carried on.

The thing is, everyone knew that a man who hadn't been able to move his legs for 40 years was now walking, jumping and DANCING, so keeping hold of the men who fixed him would've made people pretty cross.

As soon as Peter and John got out of the Temple, they went back to their mates and told them EXACTLY what had happened. It would've been pretty easy for everyone to get ANGRY or be scared but they didn't. Instead, they prayed for Peter and John.

I mean, I think I'd have been *pretty* freaked out, to be honest — but then **praying** is always a good idea.

"God, you have **ALL** the {power} you made everything, and it was <u>your</u> Holy Spirit that spoke through **David** when he said that everyone would be against the one you would send to save everyone. Just like it happened **here**, they all were against Jesus, even though (you) had sent him. And **HELP** us, God, to be brave, help us to tell people about you. God, you can make epic things happen, in the name of Jesus."

SUDDENLY, the ground "shook". Everything wibbled and wobbled in the [room] — they couldn't stand up straight and all their pictures fell off the wall. **Oops.**

The Holy Spirit filled them all up, and they started to (talk) about God in super BRAVE and extra LOUD voices.

All the people who believed in Jesus carried on sharing everything. Every single thing they owned, they ← → shared, and no one fought over anything. Can you imagine that? They even sold their HOUSES and shared out all the money. There was a guy called Joseph, who the disciples called Barney (short for Barnabas), and he sold a field and shared out the money from THAT, too. All they cared about was JESUS and telling others about everything he had done. The ones who had seen Jesus when he'd come back from the dead told everyone that he really WAS ALIVE!

CHAPTER 5

ANA, SAP & GAM

But not everyone shared everything. And that didn't go so well. AWKWARD.

There was a man named Ana (sounds like a girl's name, I KNOW, but honestly, he was a man!), who was married to Sap (weird name too, right?) and they owned a really nice house. They agreed to sell it and KEEP some of the money for themselves, I mean, how would anyone else EVER know?

SO Ana took their money to the twelve disciples and handed it over with a nice smile. He didn't say anything about the bit they'd kept for themselves, there's NO WAY Peter would be able to tell — right? WRONG.

"Why have you LiED, Ana?" said Peter. "Why did you KEEP some of the money for yourself?"

Ana looked at the floor. How did Peter know? he thought. Someone must've dropped him in it. GREAT.

"What was it that made you THINK this was OK? It's not ME you've lied to, Ana, it's GOD."

And right there and then, without even a cough or a splutter, Ana just fell down on the floor and died. Everyone stared at him for a few minutes, just to see if he was faking it, but he wasn't. It was pretty "scary", to be honest – I mean, he didn't even say anything back to Peter. He just died.

They **WRAPPED** him up, took him outside and buried him. No one really knew *WHAT* to say. Eek. ☹ ☹ ☹ ☺

A few hours later **Sap** came inside. I'm guessing she was looking for Ana – how **long** does it take to hand over a few coins?! Peter asked her how **MUCH** she and Ana had sold their house for.

She **stuck** with their 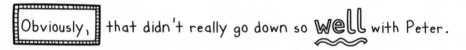 story and didn't mention the money they'd kept for themselves.

Obviously, that didn't really go down so **well** with Peter.

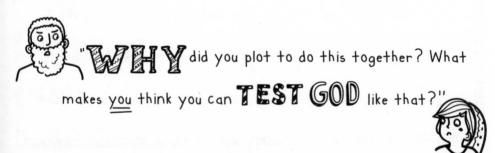

"**WHY** did you plot to do this together? What makes <u>you</u> think you can **TEST GOD** like that?"

46

Sap **SUDDENLY** realised she still hadn't (seen) Ana, and **everyone** seemed to be staring at *HER.*

"Look at those feet, Sap," said Peter.

Sap was **CONFUSED.** Why was Peter talking about feet? She looked down at her <u>own</u> feet and then noticed that Peter was pointing to the men at the **BACK** of the room.

"Those are the feet of the men who **buried** your husband, and they'll be taking **YOU** away in a moment, too."

And Sap crumpled up into a LITTLE heap on the floor, <u>just</u> like Ana had done a few hours earlier, and *THIS* time no one stood around **wondering** what to do. They just came

forward, **WRAPPED** her up, took her outside and

buried her **NEXT** to Ana.

When **everyone** heard what had happened they were

all *pretty* **FREAKED** out. Their knees knocked

and their arms **shivered**, and they remembered how

powerful God is.

God kept on doing loads of **EPIC** things through all

the people that chose to follow Jesus. The original **11** (plus

Matthias – that's the 'new' guy – remember?), well,

they got called a kind of **WEIRD** name. People

called them "**APOSTLES**".

What is an apostle? (Say "a-poss-ul".) It's actually a word Greek people would've used — except they would've said "apostolos" — and it MEANS something like "a SENT person" or "a messenger". So when everyone called the 11 + 1 "apostles" they meant that GOD had sent them and that they were bringing HIS message!

People were a LITTLE bit afraid of the apostles. They were pretty "scary". No one really felt BRAVE enough to go to the room where they were hanging out. But even though they were a bit "scary", everyone also thought they were INCREDIBLY awesomely COOL.

More and more people kept choosing to follow the way of Jesus. And they all started bringing sick people from all over the place and laying them down at the side of the road so that when Peter and the other apostles came PAST they'd get HEALED.

Well now. That all sounds pretty MARVELLOUS to me. But, don't forget about the grumpy Temple leaders — because THEY hadn't forgotten about Peter and John. If you're thinking they wouldn't be too happy, you'd be right. They were all SUPER jealous of the 11+1. How come THEY could do all these AMAZING things?

They were so peeved that they decided to put them in

prison. <u>Again</u>. They probably had their own cells by now.

But even **that** didn't help! Because, in the night, God sent an angel to unlock the prison doors and they all just walked out. The angel told them to KEEP doing what they'd been locked away for: "Tell **everyone** about the amazing kind of life JESUS has to offer," he said.

SO, that's what they did. They walked right back into the Temple and **started** talking about Jesus AGAIN.

JESUS!

The Temple leaders decided to have a <u>meeting</u>. They told the guards to BRING those Jesus people from prison, but the guards came <back and said that when they

unlocked the prison doors, Peter and his mates just weren't

there... Well, the Temple leaders just opened their

mouths and **NO WORDS**

came out. fish faces.

Then they saw someone arrive at the **BACK** of the

room and he came right over with a **message**.

"Those men that you locked up last night, they're back in

the **TEMPLE**, again telling **everyone** about

Jesus. Did **YOU** let them out?" **AWKWARD!**

The guards went outside and cornered the **APOSTLES.**

But they didn't want the CROWDS to think they

didn't like the apostles — they might start throwing

things at them if they thought THAT. So the guards

smiled sweetly, and asked the apostles nicely to go back inside.

Excoozme, Mr Apossul,

I would much like it if

inside you go again. Fanks.

"We TOLD you NOT to do this," said the Temple

leader in charge. "Stop" — go-ing — on — ab-out — Je-sus,"

he said slowly — as if Peter couldn't quite understand him.

"You are doing EXACTLY what we told you NOT

to!" Now he was clearly getting quite CROSS...

LITTLE bits of spit flew out of his mouth as he SHOUTED at them all and threw his arms in the air.

But Peter just said calmly and quietly: "We have to do what GOD tells us, not what people want. God, who has always been with us, he's the one that brought Jesus back to life after you killed him. It's THIS God that made Jesus so AWESOME. It's his plan that means Jesus is the one who can save us all, the one who can forgive us all for everything. We saw it all for ourselves, and so did the Holy Spirit. And the Holy Spirit lives inside everyone who has decided to FOLLOW God."

The Temple leaders ALL seemed to have gone a rather

funny colour. They were a kind of reddish and purplish in the face, and they LOOKED as if they might be about to POP. They were ready to finish the apostles OFF. ONCE and for ALL.

But one guy called Gam (short for Gamaliel) managed to calm things down a LITTLE. He sent all the apostles outside for a BIT, while he spoke to the leaders and told them to take a few DEEP breaths. "You need to really think about what you're going to DO with these guys. Remember what happened before with people who THOUGHT they were SPECIAL new leaders — they all just fizzled out — and everyone who followed them went away. These ones will be just the same if what they're saying is just a way for them to feel SUPER COOL – only if it is ACTUALLY God doing something AMAZING will they stay. I {think} we should just leave them alone – because what if what they're saying really is from God? You wouldn't want to fight God, would you ?"

As Gam (spoke,) their faces went from PURPLE, to RED, to pink and then back to normal. They realised he was right – just KILLING all these apostle men wasn't really going to help. But that didn't mean they'd get away with no punishment at all - OH NO.

They told the guards to bring the apostles back inside and

give them a good **BEATING**. They made <u>sure</u> every one of them ended up with plenty of CUTS and BRUISES before they let them go — and they reminded them all not to **EVER** mention Jesus again, unless they wanted a few more black eyes.

ow!

On the way out, **Peter** and all the others **THANKED** God for letting them **suffer**. That sounds *pretty* **ODD** – right? But for Peter and the others, if they were suffering because of **JESUS** then they must be doing something good.

And they carried on. **Every single day**, no matter **WHERE** they were, or **WHO** they were with, they told everyone all they **COULD** about Jesus.

CHAPTER 6

THE SPIRIT, THE WIDOWS & STEVE

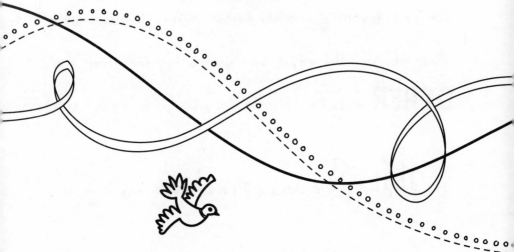

Every day, MORE and MORE people decided to follow the way of Jesus. They were ALL leaving their families and joining up as members of the big Jesus family.

That was all well and good, but lots of people had stopped looking after the people in their families who needed HELP. D'oh. USUALLY any women were cared for by everyone else in the family if their husband died. That was just the way things worked — there weren't any OTHER ways for them to get food or a place to stay.

The 11 + 1 decided a meeting was in order.

"LOOK," they said, when everyone was together.

"You can't **leave** people to go "hungry" — that's <u>not right</u>! But we can't just **STOP** telling people about God to go and deliver packed lunches. That's not right **EITHER**! **SO,** here's the plan." They told **everyone** to choose a team of **7** good and honest guys who were filled with the Holy Spirit. It would be *THEIR* job to organise food for all those who needed it, while the apostles could carry on **TEACHING** and praying.

Everyone seemed **pretty** happy with that idea, so, seven men with pretty awesome names were chosen. There was **Steve, Phil, Prochorus, Nicanor Tim, Parmenas** (no, not Parmesan cheese) and **Nico**. Once the team was <u>sorted</u>, the apostles prayed

61

for them all and sent them off on their first lunch run.

Meanwhile, more and more people kept choosing Jesus. Even some of the **TEMPLE** leaders "realised" that what they were hearing was <u>true</u> — and started to *believe*. God really blessed Steve and used him to do **AMAZING** things. But still not **everyone** could handle what they were hearing and seeing. People from all over the place often argued with Steve — they wanted him to know they couldn't **POSSIBLY** agree with the

things he was saying. But **GOD** made sure they didn't (stop)

Steve – somehow, they could never win their arguments.

So they decided the only way to get *RID* of Steve was to

hatch a **SNEAKY** plan. They rounded up some of

their **MATES** and told them to go to the Temple leaders

and say that Steve was saying really {awful} things about God.

STEVE SAID GOD HATES ME

STEVE'S A LIAR

STEVE SAID GOD SMELLS BAD

63

They **SNUCK** sssh! around following Steve, and then when he wasn't looking they **jumped** out, pounced on him and dragged him off by his hair to the Temple. Ouch. They'd thought of **everything**. They'd even managed to find

a few more people who would tell *lies* about Steve.

"He's **ALWAYS** saying awful things about the Temple."

"Yeah — that's right, he **IS**. He says Jesus is going to **TEAR** it all down."

"He says the way we've **always** done things is all **wrong**, and only **JESUS** does it right."

"What does he know? He's so RUDE."

They went ON and ON, making up one thing after another.
But Steve was super CHILLED. When the Temple leaders

looked at him they could see that he had a peaceful look on

his face. IN FACT , his face looked kind of SHINY, kind

of different, kind of... angel-like. Steve's face looked

just like an angel's face. Woah.

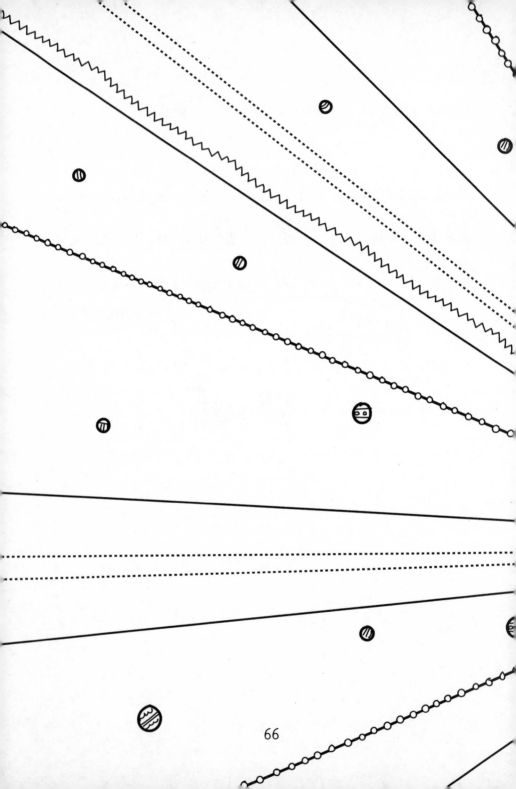

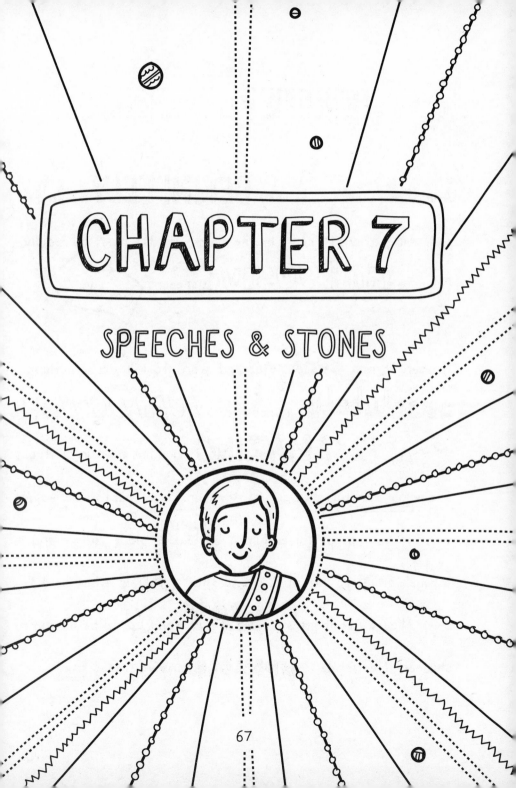

CHAPTER 7

SPEECHES & STONES

"So, is it all **TRUE?**" they said to Steve.

And I'm telling you — they **DEFINITELY** weren't

expecting Steve to reply like he did — with the most incredibly

fabulous **MAHOOSIVE** speech.

Go, Steve!

"Listen to me, **everyone**. I want to tell you something

absolutely, incredibly, *STUPENDOUSLY*,

mind-blowingly **AMAZING**. God has been in control

the whole time! Think back to Abraham. God told him to leave

everything — he promised him a **NEW** place to live and

a huge family to live in it — and that's **just** what he did.

Even though Abraham was **WAY** too **old** to be having

children, God made it **possible** anyway. God knew

that his people would struggle and suffer for a long 🕐 time, but he promised to make things right and set them free. And GUESS what? That's what he did! Abraham's son was Isaac, Isaac's son was Jacob, and Jacob had 12 sons — the 12 men who go right back to the START of our family trees."

DID YOU KNOW:

These 12 men that Steve was talking about, they're the same 12 brothers that lived hundreds and hundreds of years before. One of those brothers, Joseph, he was the one who had an amazing rainbow coat — he was the one who got stuck in a well, and then stuck in jail, and then made FRIENDS with a baker, oh and then there were cows and corn and so much more!

If you have a Bible, you can find out **more** about **Joseph** and his brothers — just open it up and look for the very FIRST book right at the beginning — it's called **GENESIS.**

"Remember Joseph — his brothers tried to get RID of him, but God rescued him and he ended up in charge of the whole of Egypt! **THEN**, when all the food ran out, Joseph's brothers NEEDED something to eat — and they heard that Egypt still had corn. SO they went to get some, and didn't even notice Joseph until they went back the NEXT time. Even though his brothers had dropped him in a well, and then sold him like he was a mouldy loaf of bread, Joseph brought them all

70

to Egypt, along with their **DAD**, Jacob, and their **Families**. They all stayed there [together] until they grew **old** and **died** and were buried back where Abraham had planned.

"**BUT** our family kept on **growing** and **growing** in Egypt, just like **GOD** had promised. Then there was a king who was **EVIL**. He tried to get *RID* of our ancestors (any) way he could. And that's when **Moses** was born — and God had a *pretty* awesome plan for Moses...

Moses? Who is he? Well, Moses was *pretty* **COOL**. When he was a baby he got involved in an amazing game of hide and seek in a little basket on a river.

He GREW up as a kind of prince, even though he wasn't really a prince, and then he RAN away after he'd done something BAD, and then he saw a bush that was on fire in the desert, and then he came < back ... If you have a BIBLE, you can find out more about Moses and everything that happened to him in a book near the beginning called Exodus.

"When Moses heard God speak through a BUSH that was on fire, but didn't burn, he fell down on the ground because he knew something AMAZING was happening. God said, 'I AM GOD. I AM the one who has always been here, I AM the one who was there with Abraham, Isaac and Jacob.' Moses was so freaked out

72

that he couldn't even LOOK at the bush any more

— and God told him to go ◁back to Egypt.

"HE would be the one whom God would use to RESCUE

his people. God had seen how much his people

had been crushed by the EVIL KING — and

Moses was the one who led the people out of

Egypt, he was the one whom God used to split the sea

in TWO and he was the one whom everyone followed in

the desert for 40 years. Moses was the ONE God

spoke to on top of a mountain in the desert, he was the ONE

who heard from God about how he wanted his people to live."

Go, Steve! Go, Steve! Everyone was listening — their faces

73

were getting **redder** and **redder** and their eyes were sticking out further and further, but Steve carried on...

"The people didn't **LISTEN**, they wanted to do things [their] way. That's when they made a baby cow out of **GOLD** and decided that it would be their **new** god. They {thought} they'd done a *pretty* good job — but God was so <u>not</u> *IMPRESSED*. He told them they'd got it **wrong** and he told them they wouldn't get to the place he'd **promised** them. But they **DID** make a sort of travel tent for God to live in that they carried through the desert **WITH** them, and then, when the time was right, Joshua led them into the **promised** place. God's travel tent stayed in the promised place until

KING David was around. But it was **KING** Solomon who made God a **PROPER** house. But don't *forget* — God doesn't <u>actually</u> live in tents or houses. It's just like Isaiah said — God lives in heaven, but he is here on earth, **TOO.** How can we make somewhere for him to live out of things that he **already** made?"

WOW. What a speech — but Steve wasn't finished there. He had an **EXTRA SPECIAL** bit to **ADD,** just for the Temple leaders...

You're all **IDIOTS,** he said. I'm *pretty* sure that didn't go down so well. I mean, you know — at least he was *HONEST...*

"You don't **really** care about God, you're always going **AGAINST** the Holy Spirit — just like people before you did. They were always trying to get **RID** of God's messengers — they killed the **VERY** people that God had sent to tell them that Jesus was on **HIS WAY**.

And now it's **YOU** — you're the **stupid** ones who betrayed God and murdered the one he sent. You're the ones who should know best and you've got it all wrong."

And then they **SNAPPED**. There was no way that Steve could say these things and get away with it. Even **NOW** he had that funny look on his face — all chilled out, like he could say whatever he wanted.

OF course, it was the Holy Spirit who was keeping Steve calm. When he looked up to God he could **SEE** JESUS standing there. Nothing could change how WONDERFUL that made him feel.

"I can **SEE** Jesus, standing there in heaven, he's right there with GOD."

The TEMPLE leaders stuck out their tongues and put their fingers in their ears and RAN at Steve; they CRUSHED around him and dragged him outside.

They picked up all the STONES they could find and threw them at Steve as HARD as they could. They threw stone after stone after stone until Steve wasn't <u>moving</u> any more.

77

The people who were watching took **OFF** their coats so they could get in on the action, and put them down in a **PILE** next to a man called Saul (I'll tell you more about him later).

Steve was praying and praying as they threw what felt like **MILLIONS** of stones at him. He asked Jesus to look after him and he knew he'd be with him **SOON**. Then, finally, Steve shouted out, "Jesus — don't hold this against them!" and then he **STOPPED** breathing.

They'd killed him.

CHAPTER 8

PETER, PONDS
& MAGIC SIMON

You **remember** that **Saul** man? The (one)
everyone threw their coats at? ➚

FACT FILE

NAME: Saul

LOCATION: From a place
called Tarsus

THINGS SAUL HATED: People who
followed Jesus

THINGS SAUL LOVED: Killing people who
followed Jesus

IMPORTANT THINGS TO REMEMBER:
Saul was Jewish, but he was also a Roman
citizen, and he was super mean

Saul was feeling rather **PLEASED** about getting

RID of Steve. He hadn't even had to do anything — the

people had just got ON with it. "At least another one of those JESUS followers is _out_ of the way," { thought } Saul.

IN FACT, to Saul, it seemed like an EXCELLENT opportunity to start hunting down the REST of those Jesus people — and that's what he did. While Steve's friends were burying him and feeling SO SAD to have lost him, Saul went on a RAMPAGE. He went into every house he could find, yanked out Jesus followers and slung them into prison.

ALL the followers (except the 11 + 1) had run away from Jerusalem. They were pretty "scared" to stay after what had happened to Steve, but they STILL wanted to tell OTHER people about Jesus. Phil (one of Steve's mates back in chapter 6) decided he'd go to a place called Samaria, and pretty soon crowds gathered around to hear what he was saying. They were proper EXCITED

when Phil got RID of evil spirits and made sick people well, and they were even more excited when they heard that Jesus didn't just come to save people in Jerusalem — but in Samaria too!

Evil spirits? <u>Spooky</u>. Well not really... In the same way that God wants to send his Holy Spirit to come and live in us and do **GOOD** stuff, sometimes, although really not too often, bad spirits get there <u>first</u>. But even **if** they manage it, Jesus always has the {power} to kick them out.

Among the **CROWDS** of people was a skinny LITTLE man with a wrinkly nose called *MAGIC* Simon. **Everyone** knew Magic Simon, he'd been around for years. He was a **magician** who could do all kinds of **DODGY** things — and he was used to everyone telling him just how **AWESOME** he was.

But Magic Simon could see that Phil had a *totally different* kind of {power.} There was something REAL, something he could almost touch about the {power} he saw in Phil. This Jesus man that Phil spoke about sounded truly incredible.

Magic Simon decided that this was something he could really believe in for himself. SO, along with everyone else in the crowd, Magic Simon was baptised.

Baptised? What's that all about? Well baptism was meant to be a sign that helped everyone SEE how a person had changed on the inside. It was a bit like having all the NASTY not nice stuff washed off and being made all clean so you could start over with GOD again. People STILL get baptised today when they choose to follow Jesus — to show that they've made a NEW start with God, too!

Afterwards, Magic Simon stuck to Phil like **glue**.

He followed him everywhere and constantly watched him.

He **EVEN** tried to follow him to the toilet AWKWARD

— but Phil managed to convince him to *politely* wait outside.

It didn't take **long** before the apostles who were back

in **J**erusalem heard about what had happened in **S**amaria.

They **decided** to send Peter and John up there so that

they could **HELP** Phil out. When they arrived, they prayed

for **everyone** to be **FILLED** with the Holy Spirit

— just like they had been (way back in chapter **2**).

(It wasn't that Phil couldn't have prayed for the Holy

Spirit to *SHOW* up, it was just that he'd baptised them

85

in the name of **JESUS** and hadn't asked the Spirit

to fill everyone up *just* yet.)

Anyway ... When Peter and John put their hands

on the heads of the **NEW** followers and asked the

Holy Spirit to come, he came in **STYLE**!

"How **much** do you want?" asked *MAGIC* **Simon**

as he poked Peter in the arm. "That hands on heads Holy

Spirit thing you're doing, (I) want to be able to do it.

It's **AWESOME!** Just name your price!

I can even pay in fish biscuits, if you'd rather..."

Peter (turned to face Magic Simon and gave him a *long*

stare. "Do you **SERIOUSLY** think you can buy gifts from God? That's not _HOW_ it works! **YOU** and your money will come to an end because you {thought} you could **pay** for God's _blessing_." Magic Simon looked at his sandals. He only wanted to be able to do what the APOSTLES were doing — they were SOOOOOO cool!

"This isn't for <u>you</u>," Peter continued, "your HEART isn't in the right place at (all.) You need to say SORRY to God for **everything** you've done that isn't what he would've wanted. You need to ask him to _forgive_ you. You're so angry about your life, you've <u>ignored</u> God for so long."

Magic Simon wrinkled up his nose and looked as if he might CRY.

"*PLEASE*, Peter, *PLEASE* tell God not to let me come to an end like you said. *PLEASE*?"

I don't **really** know what happened to Magic Simon after that. I **suppose** only **GOD** knows where he is now. But I do know that Peter and John went back down to **J**erusalem after they'd told everyone in **S**amaria all about **JESUS**.

SO, anyhow, back to Phil. God sent an angel to give Phil a message.

Hello, Phil. **GOD** says you **need** to go for a walk. Go that way, down the road through the desert to Gaza.

So he **DID**. He jumped up and began walking, right there and then. Phil *KNEW* that God would show him whatever it was he **needed** to see when the time was right. He didn't even ask why — | I mean | I think I'd like to have known where I was going... or at least how *long* I was going for. | I mean |, how many pairs of pants should I pack?

At **EXACTLY** the same time a man from **E**thiopia was just about to leave **J**erusalem in his chariot. Let's call him **Domitius** for now, or <u>Dom</u> for short. Dom worked for the **QUEEN** of **E**thiopia, looking after all her money. He found himself a *nice* comfy cushion to sit on, and settled down with a new book to read.

Phil **kept on** walking, and walking, and walking and then

all of a <u>sudden</u> the Holy Spirit spoke. "You see that chariot

over there: go over and get **NEAR.**"

It's just as well **GOD always** knows what he's doing.

Imagine just going over to a **RANDOM** chariot?!

Phil went over to the chariot, and *RAN* along next to

it. "Excuse me?" he **SHOUTED** up at the man inside.

"Excuse me? I can see you're reading a book. It sounds

a bit like Isaiah to me, do you <u>understand it all</u>?"

Dom looked down at **Phil**, rather surprised to see a

man trying to **keep up** with his chariot and have a

conversation at the SAME time.

"Erm, hi," said Dom. "Well NO, actually, I don't understand what I'm reading AT ALL. How can I possibly understand it if NO ONE explains it to me? Climb on in if you like, maybe you can TELL me all about it..."

Dom MOVED over so that Phil could share his cushion and peer over his shoulder at the book. He was indeed reading the words of God's messenger Isaiah, from hundreds and hundreds of years AGO. He was reading the bit where Isaiah talks about a sheep that is led away to be killed, but stays silent the whole time, a sheep that is laughed at by people and is NEVER really listened to.

If you have a **Bible** you can read the words that Isaiah wrote for **YOURSELF**. You can find them in the book called **Isaiah**, in chapter **53**.

"**WHY** is he talking about a sheep?" said Dom with a **CONFUSED** look on his face. "**OR** is he talking about a person who was a bit like a sheep? **OR** is he saying **he feels** like a sheep?"

"**Well**," said Phil, "let me **explain**." It took him a *while*, but Phil explained to Dom that Isaiah had been talking about **JESUS**. Even though it was hundreds and hundreds of years ago, God had told Isaiah about all the **things** that Jesus would come to do, and he'd

EVEN told him that no one would listen to him and they'd eventually kill him.

Slowly but surely, Dom began to understand what Isaiah was talking about, and as Phil told him ALL ABOUT JESUS and all the amazing things he'd done, he SUDDENLY knew it was all true. He quickly stopped his chariot, jumped out and RAN over to a small brown pond. He jumped right in and waved at Phil: "Baptise me NOW, Phil! I want to follow Jesus!" Phil jumped into the pond and DUNKED Dom under the water. As he lifted him out again Phil disappeared. Yep — I said, Phil disappeared. He was there ONE minute, and then just gone! POOF!

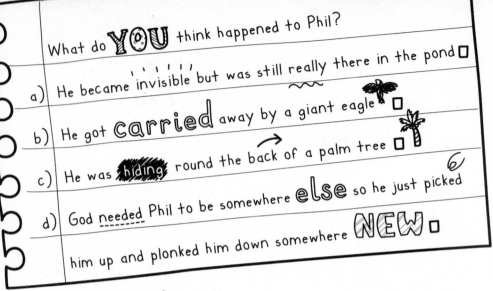

What do **YOU** think happened to Phil?

a) He became invisible but was still really there in the pond ☐

b) He got **carried** away by a giant eagle ☐

c) He was hiding round the back of a palm tree ☐

d) God needed Phil to be somewhere **else** so he just picked him up and plonked him down somewhere **NEW** ☐

Dom looked around for Phil and couldn't see him anywhere, but he was so **HAPPY** that he'd found out all about **JESUS** – that didn't seem to **matter.**

Phil opened his eyes and found himself in a place called **A**zotus. God had just picked him up from the **POND** and **PLONKED** him down here. Woah! Phil told **everyone** he met about Jesus until he came to a town called **C**aesarea. (Say see-zer-ree-er).

CHAPTER 9

BLINDING, STARVING & WEEPING

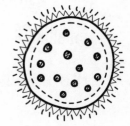

NASTY, **sneaky** Saul was getting on **pretty** well with his "Capture all Jesus people" campaign. He even went to the Temple leader and asked him to write **SPECIAL** letters giving him permission to *SNIFF* out the Jesus **followers**, tie them up and ≡drag them back to |jail| in **J**erusalem.

But on his way to **D**amascus something absolutely **INCREDIBLE** happened. The sky went white, **IN FACT**, everywhere he looked, all Saul could see was bright, **SHINY**, white light. The light was **SO BRIGHT** that it made Saul *FALL* over and try to hide his eyes.

"**Saul**! **Saul**!" said a voice. "Why are you being so

cruel to me?"

"Who are you, Lord?" whispered Saul, not <u>daring</u> to move.

"I'm **JESUS**, the one you are being so **cruel** to. Now get up and go into the **CITY** and you'll find out what you need to do **NEXT**."

Everyone on the road with Saul stood absolutely still with their eyes and mouths **WIDE** open. They'd heard the voice from ~~nowhere~~ too. They watched as Saul very *slowly* got to his feet and looked around. He waved his hands in front of his own face, and they started to wave back when they realised Saul couldn't **SEE**.

So they helped him into **D**amascus and made *SURE*

he didn't *FALL* over anything on the way. Well... not

many things. When they arrived, Saul didn't 🍴eat 🥄or drink

anything for 3 whole days, and he **STILL** couldn't see.

In **D**amascus, there was a man called **Ana** (not the

same Ana from **CHAPTER 5** – a different

one!) who *followed* Jesus. God (spoke) to him by talking

to him and showing him a picture in his head. "Ana," said

God. "I'm **here**, Lord," said Ana. "Go and find Jude's

HOUSE on Straight Street and then look inside for a man

from Tarsus called **Saul**. Right now he is praying, and

I've just shown him a picture of **YOU** standing next

to him with your hands over his eyes."

Ana didn't *quite* know what to do. He'd heard ALL about Saul and all the HORRIBLE things he did to people who *followed* Jesus.

"Erm... well the th-th-th-thing is, G-G-G-G-God," he STUTTERED, "I know what he's l-l-l-l-like. And here he even has p-p-p-p-p-ermission from the Temple leaders to c-c-c-catch p-p-p-people like me who fol-l-l-l-low you."

"It's OK, Ana," said GOD. "Just GO. I've chosen Saul to tell others about me — people who aren't Jews, people who are important like kings and queens, all SORTS of people. I will show him *everything* that he NEEDS to go through so that he can do this."

So Ana went OFF to find Saul. I reckon he must've been **SUPER** scared. I know I would've been.

When Ana got to the HOUSE there, just like GOD had said, was Saul, on his knees, praying. All of a SUDDEN, Ana didn't feel afraid any more. He went straight over and put his hands over Saul's eyes and he said, "Saul, the same Jesus that you saw on the road into the city, he sent me here so that you will see again, and be filled from the top of your head to the tip of your toes with the Holy Spirit."

Something STRANGE that looked a bit like fish skin fell out of Saul's eyes (ewww!) and then he STOOD up, jumped up and down and shouted, "I can see! I can see!"

100

He went outside and got **baptised**, and then realised how **hungry** he was! Just imagine how **hungry** you'd be if you hadn't eaten anything for 3 days...

After he'd had a rather LARGE dinner, Saul felt **much better**. He stayed in **D**amascus for a few days, and hung out with the Jesus *followers* **THERE**. He went with them to the <u>town</u> meeting place and told **everyone** he could find that Jesus was God's Son.

The crowds stared at Saul with very **CONFUSED** faces.

ISN'T HE THAT CRUEL MAN WHO KILLS JESUS PEOPLE?

I THOUGHT HE WAS HERE TO GET RID OF PEOPLE WHO FOLLOW JESUS?

WHAT'S HAPPENED TO HIM?

101

He kept on telling everyone he met that Jesus was the ONE who had been sent to save them, and he even convinced lots of Jewish people who said they'd never believe. Go, Saul!

When the Jewish LEADERS realised that people were actually listening to Saul, and that he hadn't just had a CRAZY moment where he was pretending to follow Jesus, they weren't happy with what he was doing. They weren't happy at all. They decided they'd have to KILL him. If they watched the city gates all day and all night, he'd have to come out at some point — so they'd catch him then.

But Saul found out. So his mates hid him in a giant

basket and attached it to a very **long** rope. Then they

waited until it was **dark** and lowered down their Saul-in-a-

basket over the city walls — where **no one** was watching.

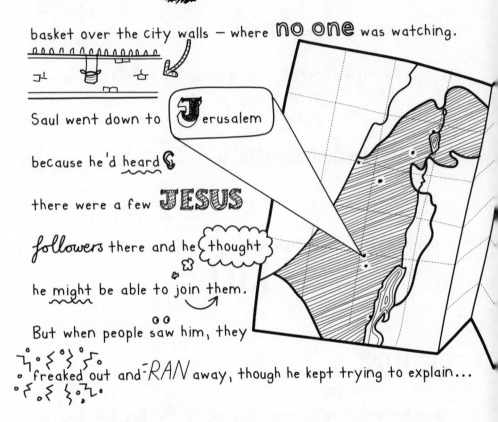

Saul went down to **J**erusalem

because he'd heard

there were a few **JESUS**

followers there and he (thought)

he might be able to join them.

But when people saw him, they

freaked out and **RAN** away, though he kept trying to explain...

But **Barnabas** listened, took Saul to meet the **11+1**

and told them everything — the **BRIGHT** light, hearing

Jesus' **VOICE**, telling everyone in **D**amascus about what God had done. When they'd heard his story, the apostles decided **Saul** was telling the truth and so he joined in with what they were doing in **J**erusalem. He even went to argue with the Greek Jews because he wanted them to **understand** that Jesus was the (only) one who could save them. But that didn't **QUITE** go to plan either — they decided they hated Saul and started to hatch a sneaky plan to **KILL** him.

THIS time, when his mates found out, they didn't put him in a basket, but they did **smuggle** him out of the city and send him down to a place called **T**arsus (that's where Saul was born, remember?).

All the Jesus *followers* left behind worked together and **HELPED** each other, and the Holy Spirit helped them to grow and stay strong. That's how the church began.

(The CHURCH? Which one? Isn't a church a building? Today, when we talk about "church", we usually think of a building. But church **isn't** a building, church is a (group) of people. When all the Jesus followers started being called "CHURCH", the word they used didn't **mean** "building", it meant "people being gathered **TOGETHER**". That's what church really is!)

As the church **GREW**, Peter moved around quite often so that he could see **everything** that was happening.

In a place called **L**ydda, he found a man who hadn't been able to get /out/ of bed for **EIGHT** years because he couldn't move — <u>at all</u>. "Jesus makes you **well** — get up and walk, make the bed!" Peter said to the man — and that's **EXACTLY** what he did. He *RAN* outside and everyone was **AMAZED** — they all knew he'd been in bed for eight years, and here he was *RUNNING* around! **WOW**! When they **realised** it was Jesus who had healed the man, they decided to *follow* him for <u>themselves</u>.

While he was [still] in Lydda, Peter heard about a woman called **Tabitha** who lived in a nearby town called **J**oppa. Tabitha *believed* in **JESUS**, and she was **always** helping others. She tried to make

106

SURE everyone in her community had what they needed. But, she had been really ill and died. When SOME of the other Jesus followers in Joppa heard that Peter was in Lydda they sent him a message asking him to come and see them QUICKLY.

As SOON as Peter got the message, he went straight to Tabitha's HOUSE in Joppa. When he got there, everyone was so upset. They even showed him some of the clothes Tabitha had made while she was still ALIVE. Peter just walked in and told them all to WAIT outside! I reckon they must've thought he was proper RUDE — but they probably forgot all about that when they saw what happened NEXT!

Peter went into the [room] where they'd put **Tabitha**. He prayed and then (told) Tabitha to get up. And she did! Woah!

Isn't that **AMAZING**! When she saw Peter she sat up and he helped her stand up. Then he went outside and told people they could come back **IN** again — and when they saw Tabitha, walking, talking and **very** alive, they told God how wonderful he was. Everyone in town soon heard about it, and decided to **believe** in Jesus for themselves.

Peter stayed in **J**oppa, and he made **FRIENDS** with a guy who made leather, called **Simon** (not Magic Simon — a **DiFFeRENT** one). Simon had a spare room, and that's where Peter hung out **for a while.**

CHAPTER 10

ANIMALS FROM THE SKY & A MAN CALLED CORNELIUS

ONE DAY, Peter was sitting on the roof of Simon's **HOUSE**, taking some time out to chat with **GOD**. After a while, his "**BELLY**" started to rumble, and he figured it was probably time for a snack. So, he got up and was just about to go downstairs when something strange happened.

Peter looked **UP** and saw a **BIG** white sheet slowly coming down from the sky. It was all lumpy, and bumpy, and **wriggly**, like there was something wrapped inside it that was moving around. It landed on the roof next to him and fell open. Inside there were lots of LITTLE animals, birds and lizards. Peter looked at the animals, and they looked at him. Then he **heard** a voice. "Peter, get up, go and **CHOOSE** an animal for your lunch." Peter said, "**NO WAY**! I'm not doing that, I've never eaten anything that God said I wasn't supposed to." The voice replied,

"If God says this food is **OK**, then (you) can't say it isn't.

If God says this food is **OK**, then (you) can't say it isn't.

If God says this food is **OK**, then (you) can't say it isn't."

And then the sheet went back to `heaven`, with all the animals WRAPPED UP inside.

Erm... How **weird** is that? Woah.

Meanwhile, in a little town further up the coast, there was a soldier called **Cornelius** who had heard about **JESUS** and was trying really hard to live like he {thought} he should. He always tried to share everything he had, and he talked with **GOD** about everything, all the time!

111

And THEN the day before Peter had his weird animal-sheet thing, Cornelius had a rather strange moment too. He saw an angel come into his room. And then it spoke: "Cornelius!" was all it said. That was enough to completely FREAK him out. "Wh-Wh-What do you want?" said Cornelius eventually.

"God has seen how GOOD and kind you have been, he knows that you really love him. Now, you need to send someone to Joppa and find a man called Peter. He's staying with Simon, the leathermaker, in a HOUSE by the sea."

When the angel had gone Cornelius found THREE men who WORKED for him and sent them straight to Joppa.

SO, that's where all of these **STRANGE** things start to make some sort of 'sense'. Well — a LITTLE bit — honestly!

Peter was **still** sat on the roof of Simon's house, trying to *figure* out what just **happened**, when three **RANDOM** men appeared. "**OI** !" They **SHOUTED**. "Is this Simon's house? Is there a guy called Peter staying here?" Peter was still totally **LOST** in his thoughts, trying to *figure* out what had happened, when the Holy Spirit interrupted him, and said: "**Peter**, there are three men down there looking for **YOU**. Go and say 'Hi' — I've sent them here on purpose!"

Peter **SHOOK** his head, snapped out of his thoughts

and §*RAN* down the steps. "Hi! — I think it's me you're looking for. How can I **HELP**?"

"Cornelius told us to find you," they said. "He loves GOD and everyone knows he's a good man. An angel told him to tell (us) to tell (you) that you **NEED** to come ⬅️back with us to Cornelius' house so that he can *listen* to you."

"OH, OK," said Peter. "Why don't you come **IN** and stay for a bit? I've got plenty of tasty snacks. I'm sure Simon won't mind. And then we can get going in the morning."

SO, the **NEXT** day they started the rather *long* walk to Caesarea. Quite a **FEW** of the Jesus people from Joppa came along too. When they **eventually** arrived at Cornelius' **HOUSE**, with very tired feet and "rumbly" bellies, a whole **CROWD** of people were waiting for them.

Cornelius had told his **brother**, *Hi!* and his [other] **brother**, and his **dad**, and his **mum**, and his **aunt** and **uncle** and his [other] **uncle**, and his friend **Dave**, *HEY!* and his other friend **Bob** that Peter was coming. They were all trying to get **OUT** of the front door at the same time when they **SAW** Peter and the others arriving.

Cornelius made it out first and ran out to say Hi to Peter. But he didn't JUST say "Hi" — he fell down and WRAPPED himself around Peter's feet. "Oh, Peter, you're AMAZING," he said. Then, realising he might look a little silly, he said, "I'm honoured to meet you, SIR Peter," in a very deep and serious voice.

"Get OFF! My feet probably stink!" said Peter with a smile. "I'm just a man, come on, stand up! I'm nothing special!"

Cornelius, who was looking a little sheepish now, led Peter and the others inside. Peter couldn't quite believe how many people had SQUEEZED into such a small room — just so that they could hear what he had to say.

116

"You all know that (Jews) and (Gentiles) don't mix — right?

But GOD told me that's not how it works any more. That's WHY I came straight away when these men told me you'd asked for me. So... EXACTLY what did you WANT me for, anyway?"

"Well..." said Cornelius, "four days ago I was praying at three in the afternoon, and then this rather scary giant glowman appeared in my house. I'm pretty sure he was an angel, because he brought me a message from God. He told me that God had seen how much I love him, and then he told me to find you, and said you were in Simon's house in Joppa, by the sea.

117

So I sent these men to **FIND** you, and well, now you're **HERE**. And we're all ready and waiting to see what **GOD** wants to say through you."

What is a **GENTILE**? Well, a Gentile isn't a **SPECIAL** sort of gentle person with an extra 'i', a Gentile is **basically** anyone who isn't a Jew. Well, what **IS** a Jew, you might be wondering? A Jew is a person who **believes** in God, and who **FOLLOWS** him according to all the rules that he made before Jesus came. Jewish people go **all the way** back to Abraham and his son Isaac, and his son Jacob, and their descendants became known as Jews. Anyhow, Jews and Gentiles weren't **supposed** to mix because the

Jews {thought} that the Gentiles weren't very CLEAN — but that wasn't because they didn't have a bath often enough, it was because the JEWS didn't think the GENTILES were part of God's chosen people.

SO Peter sat down in the middle of the LITTLE room and began to talk.

"God loves everyone. Anyone who FOLLOWS him makes him happy. It doesn't matter where you're from — he's there for ALL of you. REMEMBER the message he sent through Jesus — he told us he was God for everyone. Every single person! After Jesus was baptised and filled with the Holy Spirit he did AMAZING things – he **HEALED** people who were ill, he got rid of **evil** spirits, he did so many awesome things because God was **WITH** him. We saw **WHAT** he did, and we saw **HOW** he died. We saw how people didn't **listen** to him and how they wanted to get *RID* of him. We saw how they killed him by nailing him to a cross – and we saw how he was buried in a tomb. And then..."

Peter jumped up and started to get super excited...

"And then... We saw him come **BACK** to life!" Peter fist-pumped the *AIR* and made an excited LITTLE squeaky noise.

"And that's all because God is so **EPIC**. It was God that brought him **BACK**, it was God that let us see him and eat breakfast on the BEACH with him. And it

was GOD who told us that we had to tell everyone

that HE IS GOD and he is AWESOME,

and that anyone who chooses to believe in him and follow

his ways will be forgiven."

Everyone listened to Peter as if they'd NEVER

heard anything more important in their lives. No one had

moved, and everyone's eyes stayed on Peter's face

the whole time. While he was talking, the Holy Spirit showed

up and filled every person in the ROOM. They ALL

started speaking in DIFFERENT languages and

SHOUTING out to God, telling him how incredible he is.

Peter's **mates** from Joppa just [stared] and [stared] —
the Holy Spirit had FILLED people who weren't even
Jews. Woah! What Peter was saying *MUST* be true!

"SEE!" said Peter. "Who can (stop) God filling those
he <u>wants</u> to FILL? Who can stop them being baptised?!"

Everyone piled outside to LOOK for some water,
and all Cornelius' friends and family were
baptised in a LITTLE pond.

Cornelius was SO happy that he asked Peter and his friends
to STAY with them for a <u>week</u> or <u>two</u>.

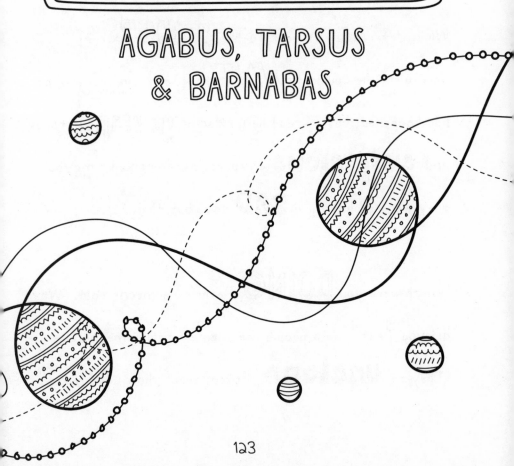

CHAPTER 11

AGABUS, TARSUS & BARNABAS

Sooo... Back in Jerusalem the apostles heard what Peter had been up to, and they {thought} it was really rather dodgy that Gentiles had become Jesus followers. AWKWARD. For Peter anyway.

When Peter made it back to the OTHERS in Jerusalem, he couldn't WAIT to {tell} everyone what had happened, but instead he met some grumpy stares and suspicious whispers. Peter thought maybe they were all having a BAD day, but then...

"What were you DOING, Peter?" someone said. "Why did you ¥eat⸱ with people like them?" said someone else. "They're unclean, Peter, eurgh, how could you?"

"Listen," said Peter. "They're not **unclean**, they're just like **YOU** and **ME**, they're God's people too! God *TOLD* me so.

"When I was in **J**oppa, I saw something **really, really** weird when I was chatting to **GOD** one day. There was a sheet that came down from heaven with loads of animals **WRAPPED** in it. A voice said to me that I was **supposed** to choose one and eat it for my lunch – kill it and eat it. But I said **NO** because that's not how God would want me to do things. But then the **voice** said, if God says it's **OK** to eat this food, then it's **OK**. It happened **3** times in a row, and then the sheet and the animals went back the way they'd come.

I didn't really know what was GOING ON, but then some men turned up and told me they had been sent to find me. The Holy Spirit told me to go with them, and I did, all the way to Caesarea, and the Holy Spirit also told me (and this is the really IMPORTANT bit!) that I shouldn't treat people (any) differently from one another, no matter whether they were like me or not like me."

Everyone looked a bit more INTERESTED now — this 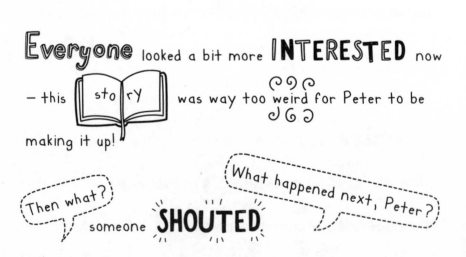 story was way too weird for Peter to be making it up!

Then what? someone SHOUTED. What happened next, Peter?

"So I went down to Caesarea to a HOUSE that belonged to a man called Cornelius. These guys here, they came TOO, they saw it ALL." Peter pointed at his mates in the CROWD that had followed him from Joppa to Caesarea.

"Anyway, when I met Cornelius, it turns out that God had been speaking to him. He'd sent an angel to tell him that he had to find me so that I could come and talk to him and his friends and his family (he had a BIG family!) about JESUS. So that's what I did — and when I was talking, the Holy Spirit just showed up all by himself and FILLED everyone who was there. It was just like when it happened to us for the first time.

Then I remembered what Jesus said about John baptising people with water, but that he would baptise people with the Holy Spirit. You see — God blessed these people just like he blessed US. Because we ALL believe in Jesus. How can I be the one to decide who GOD loves? Of course I can't — it's up to him!"

The INTERESTED faces had turned into surprised faces, with wide open mouths and staring eyes. No one spoke for a while, and then one after another they began to shout out to GOD, telling him how wonderful and awesome he is.

"God even loves the Gentiles enough to make a way for them to be forgiven. WOW! WOW! WOW!

128

He's more AMAZING than I ever imagined..."

Anyway. You remember, a while back I (told) you

about a LOAD of Jesus followers who ended up all over

the countryside because they didn't want to get caught and

put in prison, or get stones thrown at them like Steve?

Well, in case you've been wondering what happened

to them, I {thought} I'd tell you.

SO. These Jesus FOLLOWERS hadn't heard

about what Peter had been doing, and they wouldn't

tell anyone about Jesus unless they were Jewish. But God

was {still} with them, and {still} HELPED them

to tell all the Jews they met about Jesus and all that

he had DONE. Loads and loads of people who heard about Jesus chose to believe and decided to follow him for themselves.

As usual, the apostles in Jerusalem heard about what was going on and decided to send Barnabas to a city called ANTIOCH. Barnabas was SO excited when he saw how many NEW followers there were and he told them all to stay STRONG in their new faith. Barnabas was a GREAT GUY. And it was almost as if he was so full of the Holy Spirit that he oozed his love of Jesus everywhere he went.

After he'd been in ANTIOCH for a while, Barney decided to go to Tarsus and look for Saul. You

FACT FILE

NAME: Barnabas (aka Barney), except before his name was Barnabas it was Joseph

LOCATION: Jerusalem

INTERESTING THING: Barnabas was a Greek Jew, and he was especially good at encouraging people to stay strong in their faith — which is super cool, because his name means "Son of Encouragement"!

remember Saul — right? The JESUS follower killing guy, who saw a BRIGHT light, fell over, heard Jesus speak to him, went blind, got SUPER hungry, got his sight back, ate a BIG dinner and now couldn't stop telling people about Jesus? Well, that's who Barney was looking for.

Barney found Saul and took him ← back to ANTIOCH so that they could both **support** the new church that was starting to **GROW** there. They stayed for a whole **YEAR** encouraging people and helping them to stay strong in their *faith.*

After a while, the Jesus followers in **ANTIOCH** got a bit of a **name** for themselves. No one had really known what they were **supposed** to call them up until now: Jesus **FOLLOWERS**? Jesus **PEOPLE**? **APOSTLES**? None of these quite seemed to work — and that's when the people who followed → **JESUS** started to be called **CHRISTIANS.**

(Why Christians? Have you ever wondered why Christians are called Christians, not just Jesus followers, or Jesusites or something? Well, apart from the fact that Jesus followers takes longer to say, CHRISTIANS kind of makes sense. Jesus was quite OFTEN called Jesus Christ, or just The Christ — which is because the word "Christ" means "the chosen one". And THAT'S who Jesus was — God's chosen one. So Christ-ians aren't people who looked a bit like Jesus but were actually called Ian, they're people who believe in Jesus Christ and FOLLOW his ways.)

The church in ANTIOCH got bigger and bigger, and

God sent messengers to them from Jerusalem. One man called Agabus was FULL of the Holy Spirit and told the Christians in ANTIOCH all kinds of things that were going to happen in the future — and they ACTUALLY did happen!

Barney and Saul took money and supplies with them from ANTIOCH to all the other believers in the area. The church in ANTIOCH wanted to share everything they had so that MORE and MORE people would hear about JESUS.

CHAPTER 12

WORMS, WORRY & WONDER

Since Saul was now a GOOD GUY, you might be wondering if there were still any BAD guys.

Well, let me tell you, there absolutely, definitely, TOTALLY were.

KING Herod was a seriously BAD guy. He hated people who were part of this new CHURCH thing. He caught one of the apostles called James and chopped his head OFF with a sword. BLEURGH. But WORSE than that, when he noticed that some of the Jews thought that chopping James' head off was a GOOD idea, he decided to CATCH Peter...

But don't WORRY — Peter didn't get his head chopped

off straight away. Herod put him in prison instead because everyone was busy celebrating the PASSOVER FESTIVAL, so no one would be interested in what happened to Peter's head.

(The Passover Festival? What were they CELEBRATING? Find out more with a Bible in Exodus 12.)

Herod really, really, really didn't want Peter to escape, though. That'd make him look pretty stupid. So he chained him up and put four sets of soldiers outside his prison cell on GUARD. But when the church found out that Peter had been captured and locked up in prison, they prayed and prayed and prayed.

What do you think happened **NEXT**?

a) Peter had **his** head chopped off ☐

b) Peter [stayed] in prison ☐

c) Peter escaped from prison when the guards weren't looking ☐

d) Peter walked out of prison and the guards just watched ☐

On Peter's *LAST* night in prison, before Herod was going to erm... well, you know...**Anyway**, Peter was *trying* to get some sleep, which was kind of **AWKWARD** since he was lying on the floor with a soldier on each side of him. But **eventually** he nodded off.

After a while, one of them poked him. That was seriously annoying. Peter poked him back. But then he

138

felt the OTHER one poke him. So he rolled over to

poke that one BACK. But when he opened his eyes he saw

a glowing man standing above him. He was the one

who'd been doing the poking! The soldiers were still snoring

their HEADS OFF. Even though it was the middle of

the night, the cell was super BRIGHT, and Peter had to

squint just to see the man standing there. Peter thought

he must be DREAMING, but it was a pretty

AWESOME dream, so he let it carry on...

Peter was just thinking that the glowing man was

probably an angel, when it spoke. "Hello! You need

to get up, QUICK, now!" And when Peter stood up the

chains around his arms and legs just fell OFF, and the

zzzzzzzzzzz

snoring soldiers didn't even *NOTICE*! They just **kept on** snoring.

"Put your belt on, and don't *forget* your coat," said the angel, "and now let's get *OUT* of here!"

Peter *FOLLOWED* the glowing man down lots of **TWISTY**, turny corridors, past loads of soldiers who looked very awake, but didn't seem to (see) Peter and his **NEW** glow-friend. ODD — but awesome, right?!

When they arrived at the **BIG** prison gate, it just opened all by itself and they walked right through. "This is

AMAZING! Thanks for getting me out, how did you do it?" asked Peter as they walked down the road. But, when he turned around to see why his glow-friend hadn't replied, he couldn't SEE him anywhere. He'd just disappeared. No way!

Peter "shivered." It was like he'd woken UP from the most awesome (dream) — except it wasn't a dream, because he was still standing in the middle of the road, not far from the big prison gate. God really had sent an angel to bust him out of prison and protect him from Herod! EPIC!

Realising QUICKLY that he couldn't just stand there in the middle of the road in the dark, Peter figured out that he must be NEAR Mark's mum's HOUSE. If he could find his way there then hopefully she'd let him in and he could DECIDE what to do next.

What Peter didn't know was that loads of people were already in Mark's mum's house. They'd been there ALL night, praying that Peter would be /let/ out of prison. So when he arrived and knocked on the door Rhoda (she worked for Mark's mum) was SO EXCITED that she shut the door in his face and RAN back inside, SQUEALING and jumping up and down, and said, "It's Peter! He's here. Outside. NOW!"

"Don't be silly. He's in prison, Rhoda Maybe it's just someone who LOOKS like him, or maybe it's an angel," they all said. "I **know** he was in prison," she gasped, "but now he's not in prison. He's here! At our house!"

Meanwhile, Peter was still stood outside the door. He was quite **COLD** now, and he just wanted somewhere to get **warm**. So he kept knocking... Eventually, a **FEW** people went out together to see who was still knocking on the door, and when they opened it and saw Peter they all **SQUEALED** and jumped up and down too!

"Sssssssssshhh!" said Peter as he **SQUEEZED** through the door past the jumping people. "It's alright, **GOD** sent an angel to get me!" And, when he finally got them to be quiet and **listen**, he told them the whole story.

"Tell everyone what has happened, and all that GOD has done," said Peter. Then he got up to GO, just before the sun came up...

In the MORNING, the soldiers in the prison were horrified to see that Peter wasn't in his cell. "Did you let him out?" "Did you fall asleep when you were zzzzzzzz supposed to be watching him?" "Where is he?" They knew Herod would go MAD when he found out — and he did. He kept on asking them questions ??? that they couldn't answer and so, in the end, he was SO annoyed he just decided to kill them all. What a lovely man...

Then, feeling very grumpy, Herod went off to

144

Caesarea, wearing a very large frown. IN FACT Herod was just **grumpy** all the time. Everyone annoyed him, and he didn't care about anyone but himself. Some people from a nearby town, that Herod had fallen out with, came to **SEE** if they could get him to make up with them. They **really** needed him to be *nice* to them, because he looked after all their FOOD – and if he was in a **BAD** mood, then they were going to be *SERIOUSLY* hungry.

Herod sat on his **BIG COMFY** chair and looked down at them all, and realised they were **SHOUTING** something at him.

You think you're a god, not a man!

Herod didn't *MIND* them shouting that. <u>I mean,</u> after all, he **was** like a god, **wasn't** he?

Erm... **NO**. And right [there] and [then] God [sent] an [angel] to get rid of Herod, who fell off his chair, flopped onto the floor and died. End. Of. Herod. And then a **GREAT BIG** pile of worms appeared and gobbled him up. **Ewwww**. I don't imagine he would've tasted very *nice* — not even as worm food. **BLEURGH**.

Even though Herod had tried **really** hard to [stop] them, Barnabas and Paul had helped the church to keep on growing. But [after a while,] they decided it was time to go [back] to Jerusalem, and this time, they took Mark with them.

CHAPTER 13

EVIL ELLY & THE PEEVED JEWS

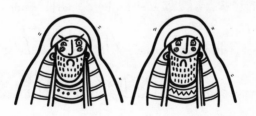

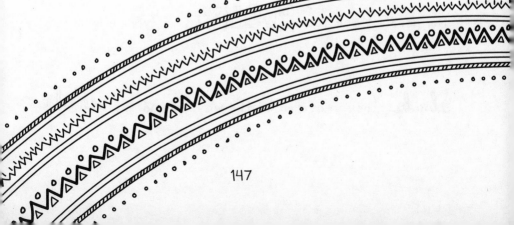

Barney and Saul ended up in ANTIOCH, and while they were there, God (spoke) to some of the church leaders. He TOLD them to pray and then send Saul and Barney out on a NEW journey — so they did!

The Holy Spirit sent Barney and Saul on a <u>boat</u> to Cyprus. They took John (who was sometimes called Mark — a bit CONFUSING — right?) with them so that he could help out, and when they ARRIVED they told all the Jews they could FIND about JESUS.

They even went into the town meeting places and told the people there too. RISKY!

Slowly, they travelled all the way around the whole

island, and everything was going *pretty* well until they met a man called ELYMAS (I'm going to call him Elly), with a long white beard, in a place called Paphos (say Pa-foss). Elly was a magician. He worked for a very IMPORTANT and clever man who wanted to hear what Saul and Barney had to say.

But Elly didn't want his BOSS to hear anything about Jesus or all the things he'd done. Er... MEAN!

But the Holy Spirit showed Paul just what Elly was like.

149

(Paul? Don't you mean Saul? You might be thinking I've just made a spelling MISTAKE. But I haven't. You see Saul was also known as Paul. CONFUSING? Yep, I know. But let me explain... You remember I said before that Saul was kind of INTERESTING, because not only was he a Jew, but he was also a Roman? Well, his JEWISH name was Saul, but his Roman name was Paul. So... Saul = Paul – got it? Anyway, from now on Saul stopped calling himself Saul and starting ONLY using Paul, so that's what I'm going to do too!)

"You are an evil man," said Paul. "You don't care about things being RIGHT; you're a LIAR and a cheat. You don't want to lead people to the one true God, you want to lead them **away** from him." Elly stood

there with his hands on his hips, looking like he **really**

couldn't care **LESS**, with a **nasty** smirk on his face.

But God sees you, said Paul.

Elly's smirk twitched a LITTLE bit, but he didn't *MOVE*

an **INCH** and didn't say a word.

"Because you are against **GOD**, he is against you.

Because you **TRIED** to stop people from seeing him,

he's going to stop **YOU** from seeing at all."

Elly's smirk disappeared completely as he realised he couldn't

see any more. He started *RUNNING* around with

his arms stretched out in front of him, "BUMPING" into things and "SHOUTING" for someone to come and hold his hand.

When Elly's boss SAW what had happened, he instantly decided that what Paul and Barney had been talking about was REAL. He decided to follow Jesus for himself.

Paul and Barney left Cyprus on another boat. This time they were heading for a place called Perga, which was about 120 miles north of where they were, and back on the mainland. But John, who'd been following them all the way round Cyprus to Perga, decided it was time go back to Jerusalem. Maybe he was getting homesick...

When they'd arrived back on the mainland, Paul and Barney travelled to ANTIOCH (no, not the place they had been before, a different ANTIOCH — maybe someone got bored when they were thinking up place names). They found a local Jewish meeting place and went inside. The people there were in the middle of listening to some of the words GOD had spoken through his messengers hundreds of years before, and afterwards the Jewish leaders invited Paul and Barney to speak to everyone. I'm not sure they really KNEW what they were letting themselves in for. "Your God, the AWESOME one, the one you love, he is the same God that led his people out of Egypt. He is the one that looked after them in the desert for 40 YEARS, even when they complained! He kept his promises

153

and LED them to a new land they could call their OWN, where they stayed for HUNDREDS of years. And then he SENT people to lead them and judge them, and then he sent people to them as his messengers.

"He put kings on the throne like DAVID. God said: 'David is a man with a HEART like mine who will do what I want.' Lots and lots and lots and lots of years after David, God sent JESUS to save us, just like he said he would. John was sent before Jesus to tell everyone that God's Saviour was on the way, and John was the one who baptised people when they wanted to turn back to God. John told everyone that HE wasn't the one who would save them, JUST that he wanted them to know that **JESUS**, the one who would be **SPECIAL**, was coming."

Everyone still seemed to be *listening*, even though a **FEW** frowns were appearing in the **CROWDS**.

But Paul carried on...

"So John had told **everyone** that Jesus was coming, and that he was <u>seriously</u> important, but even when he *CAME* people just didn't **GET** it. It was as if they couldn't see him, or <u>understand</u> **anything** he said, or what God's messengers had been saying about him **ALL ALONG**. And in the <u>end</u> they just wanted to get *RID* of him. So they made a SUPER sneaky plan, to catch Jesus

and kill him, even though he'd done NOTHING wrong.

When everything had happened, just like God said it would,

they buried Jesus in a (tomb) and rolled a big stone in

front of the door. But this is where it gets SUPER

AWESOME because Jesus didn't stay dead —

he came back to life! Loads of people saw him, and they're

the ones who KEEP telling everyone about him. And

that's what we're doing too!

"All along God has KEPT his promises, he sent

Jesus to us and, because he brought Jesus back to life again,

it proves he has power over death. When KING David

died all those years ago, he stayed dead, even though he

was a man who lived FOR God. But not JESUS.

Just like David said, God PROVED through Jesus that

death [isn't] the end! It's only because of Jesus that we can

be forgiven and find a way <back] to God. Jesus carried

all of our sins FOR US so that we don't have to carry

them. All the things we've done that go against GOD –

Jesus has taken them all away. It wouldn't have

mattered how HARD we'd tried to get rid of them

ourselves, (we) could never have done it – only Jesus can!"

(What is SIN ? Christians talk about sin all the

time. Maybe TOO MUCH of the time, actually...

But what even IS IT ? Basically, sin is just a fancy

word for saying "not loving God properly". A sin is a

thought, an **ACTION**, a word, or anything that we do that God wouldn't want. The trouble with sin is that it gets in the WAY of a GOOD relationship with GOD, because God really doesn't <u>like</u> sin. But the GREAT thing is that he loves us and so he wants to forgive us and start over.)

Paul and Barney looked down at the CROWDS. There were wide open eyes, open mouths, frowny faces and waving hands. Barney could see that people were muttering

? ? ? ?

to each other and asking questions, but lots of them looked SO, SO, SO excited!

"So make SURe," continued Paul, "that you don't end up

like the OTHERS. Don't ignore Jesus – don't TRY to get rid of him, believe!"

Paul and Barney started to make their way outside, but it was pretty DIFFICULT. Everyone kept PUSHING and SHOVING and trying to get to them.

"Oi! Paul! Don't go! Tell us more!" "Hey, Barney – come back NEXT week will you?!" "Do you like fish biscuits, Paul?"

Even when they made it out of the door, loads of people from the crowds just kept on following them, and even some of the Jews decided Paul and Barney were worth listening to and they were EXCITED by what they had to say.

And SURE ENOUGH, Paul and Barney did turn up again NEXT Saturday, and pretty much everyone in the whole town was trying to >squeeze< themselves to the FRONT of the crowd and hear Paul and Barney speak. Well, not QUITE everyone...

You see some of the Jews were RATHER peeved that everyone was listening to Paul and Barney and not to them. IN FACT, they were very, very jealous. So they decided to (tell) everyone that Paul and Barney were wrong, and said all kinds of nasty things about them.

x x x

x x x

MEAN.

But Paul and Barney didn't SEEM to care. They just smiled and said, "Well, we've TOLD you what God

160

wanted you to hear — if you {think} you're not GOOD enough for GOD, if you {think} what we say isn't true, then we'll just talk to the Gentiles INSTEAD.

"God has told us to be like a LIGHT to the Gentiles, to show them the way to JESUS, so that he can save them."

This made the Gentiles SUPER happy, of course, and they all jumped up and down and shouted out to God, telling him how AWESOME he is. Loads of them decided they would follow Jesus for themselves, and they told all their friends, who told all their friends, who told all their friends, and the message about Jesus

spread *FURTHER* and *FURTHER* and *FURTHER*!

But when the peeved Jews found out what was going on they were, well, even **more** peeved. So they carried on telling BIGGER and BIGGER lies about Paul and Barney and saying **horrible** things about them. They <u>even</u> went to see all the important city people and told them that Paul and Barney were TROUBLEMAKERS.

It got <u>so bad</u> in the end that Paul and Barney had to leave ANTIOCH, but they knew they'd done what they came to do and so just moved on to a NEW town. The Holy Spirit looked after them and helped them to stay strong and full of joy, even when things were seriously hard.

CHAPTER 14

PISIDIA, ATTALIA & WHATJAMACALLIA?

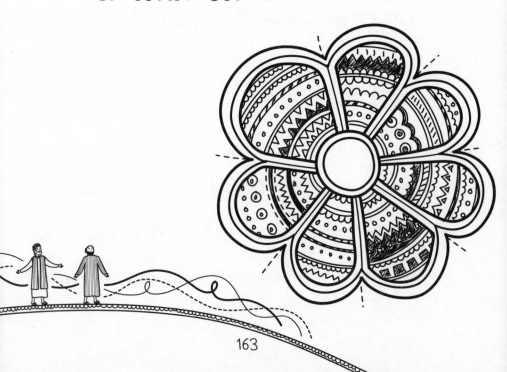

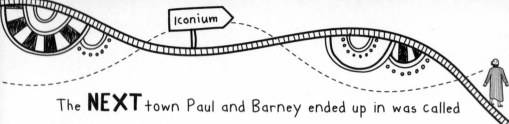

Iconium

The **NEXT** town Paul and Barney ended up in was called 1conium (say eye-cone-ee-um), and they did <u>exactly</u> what they'd done in ANTIOCH. They went to the ✡ Jewish meeting place and told **everyone** who would *listen* about Jesus, and LOADS of those who heard decided to **believe** for themselves. But even though they were in a new town, there were still PLENTY of ~~scribbled out~~ peeved Jews around who were ⌐soon¬ up to their usual tricks.

Paul and Barney had only been there for a **few** days when they heard that the *PEEVED* Jews had started saying all kinds of **RIDICULOUS** things about them. But this time, Paul and Barney didn't **leave**, they just stayed even *longer* and shouted even louder about how awesome

164

Jesus is, and God used them to do some _really_ amazing things.

Some people in Iconium loved Paul and Barney and followed them **everywhere**, but other people _believed_ everything the peeved Jews said, and they hatched a sneaky LITTLE plan.

Some of the Jewish and Gentile leaders who didn't _like_ Paul and Barney decided to corner them, and _TRY_ to throw rocks at them until they couldn't **move** any more.

NICE.

BUT Paul and Barney **HEARD** what they were planning and decided they really would have to _RUN_ away this time. **SO**, they went on to the **NEXT** town, and then the **NEXT** town, and then the one after _that_, and they **kept on** telling people all about **JESUS.**

In a place called **L**ystra (say List-rah) Paul and Barney found a man sitting at the **SIDE** of the road. His legs were all **WONKY** and didn't work at all.

When Paul and Barney sat down **NEXT** to him and started talking to him, the man stared at them. People usually just **ignored** him, or fell over his legs, or told him he was in the **WAY**. They certainly didn't sit down, have a chat and tell him some truly **AMAZING** things.

(Hi, man!)

While Paul was speaking to the man with the **WONKY** legs, he looked him right in the (face) and he could see that the man **really, really** wanted to walk, and he saw that the man really *believed* that Jesus could heal him.

SO Paul jumped up and said, "**UP** you get, on your feet!" And the man who'd **never** walked jumped right up and starting walking around! **WOAH!**

ALL the people who had been walking past the man **every day** saw that his legs were working, they saw him walking and jumping *up and down*, they thought it was absolutely amazing! Only, they didn't *QUITE* seem to understand that it was **GOD** who had made the man well again... so they {thought} that **Paul** and **Barney** must be human versions of gods.

They started called Barney "Zeus" (say Zoows), and they called Paul "Hermes" (say Her-mees).

(ZEUS and HERMES? What? The people in Lystra believed in lots of different gods. They thought there was a god for **everything**. Zeus was meant to be a *god* of thunder and lightning who was in charge of a bunch of **OTHER** gods. Hermes was meant to be the *god* of in-between places, and the people in Lystra thought that Hermes was the one who brought messages from other gods. It was all a bit **CONFUSING**, and when Paul and Barney talked about (one) God, the people couldn't **QUITE** get their heads (round it. errrr... Which **GOD** did they mean? It took them a **while** to get the right idea...)

Hmmm... Just one..?

People even started to bring cows and flowers and all (kinds of things to Paul and Barney as special presents.

When Zeus and Hermes, **NO**, I mean Barney and Paul,

figured out what was happening they went a LITTLE bit

crazy. They ripped **ALL** their clothes and

SHOUTED at everyone.

"We're **NOT** gods, we're just Paul and Barney. We're

just like you. We came here to tell you about the one

TRUE GOD ♡ who loves you — the one who sent

his Son Jesus to die for you and take away your sins.

These gods you believe in, they don't mean anything

to the one **TRUE GOD**. He's the (one) who made

everything you can **SEE** ! He's the (one) who

sends the (rain) and gives you food, he's the (one) who

makes you happy!"

But people kept on bringing **SPECIAL**. presents to Paul and Barney, and they ended up surrounded by **RANDOM** animals, spiky plants, hundreds of fish biscuits, **SUPER** posh clothes and **more**!

It didn't last **long**, though, because when the peeved Jews from **I**conium and **ANTIOCH** heard what was going on they came straight ⟫ to **L**ystra and told **everyone** that Paul and Barney were **EVIL**. They weren't gods at all, and what they were saying about this **JESUS** character — well that was all **lies**. They managed to convince **everyone** in **L**ystra, and **that** was when their sneaky stone-throwing plan launched into **ACTION**.

Before Paul could escape,

the CROWDS grabbed him

and threw BIG stones at him

until he couldn't move any more. Then they DRAGGED

him outside the town — they were pretty sure

they'd killed him, and they were feeling rather pleased with

themselves. So they just LEFT him lying there

and walked away with SMUG faces.

But Paul wasn't DEAD, and when the Jesus followers

found him and prayed for him he got UP and went back

into town. In the morning, Paul and Barnabas moved

on to the NEXT town, where people were really keen

to hear about Jesus and lots of people chose to follow him.

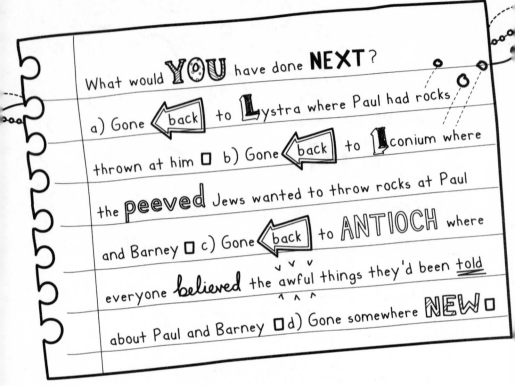

What would **YOU** have done **NEXT**?

a) Gone ⟨back⟩ to **L**ystra where Paul had rocks thrown at him ☐ b) Gone ⟨back⟩ to **I**conium where the **peeved** Jews wanted to throw rocks at Paul and Barney ☐ c) Gone ⟨back⟩ to **ANTIOCH** where everyone **believed** the awful things they'd been <u>told</u> about Paul and Barney ☐ d) Gone somewhere **NEW** ☐

Paul and Barney **decided** that first of all they'd go back to **L**ystra. (They were <u>obviously</u> feeling ´extra´ **BRAVE** that day!) After they'd been to **L**ystra they went back to **I**conium and then they went ⟨back⟩ to **ANTIOCH**. (Meeting people who wanted to throw ⟨rocks⟩ at them didn't seem to put them **OFF!**)

In **each town** they visited, they met up with the Jesus **followers** there and encouraged them to be **BRAVE**.

"If people make life *DIFFICULT* for you because you **follow** Jesus, just keep on **believing**. God has wonderful things _waiting_ for you," they said. Paul and Barney chose **LEADERS** for each church and then spent some time praying for them, asking **GOD** to look after them and keep them **STRONG**.

On their way back to **ANTIOCH** Paul and Barney went through **some** places with very **STRANGE** names like [Pisidia,] [Perga,] [Attalia] and **PLENTY** more 'Whatjamacallia' places that I can't remember how to spell!

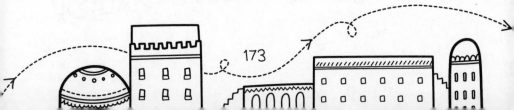

While they'd been AWAY, the church they'd left behind in ANTIOCH (that's the first ANTIOCH in chapter 11 and at the beginning of chapter 13, not the other one!) had been praying for Paul and Barney, asking GOD to HELP them in all they did. When they got there, Paul and Barney spent AGES telling everyone about everything that had happened — all the people they'd met, all the places they'd been, how many Gentiles now believed in Jesus and how AMAZING it all was.

And FINALLY, Paul and Barney took a pause for a while. I think they needed time to recover from all their over EXCITING ADVENTURES!

CHAPTER 15

ITCHY FEET &
ARROGANT PEOPLE

But the pause didn't last for *long*. Paul and Barney

ended up in a **BIG** argument with some SUPER

annoying arrogant people who turned up and started telling

everyone that **NO ONE** could really follow

Jesus unless they *followed* every single one of

the Old rules that God gave to Moses.

It didn't seem to MATTER how many times Paul

and Barney told them that Jesus wanted to SAVE

everyone — whether they were following the rules or not

— the arrogant people just **SHOUTED** their ideas

even LOUDER.

Eventually, Paul and Barney and a few others

went to see the apostles in Jerusalem. On the WAY

there, they told people about the Gentiles who now *believed*

in JESUS. It made everyone super happy.

When they ARRIVED, Paul and Barney told the

apostles everything that had been happening, and

all about the arrogant people. They {thought} everyone

would AGREE with them and that'd be that.

But nooooooooooo...

SOME of the Jesus followers were arrogant people

as well, and said that everyone who wanted to *follow*

Jesus DID have to follow all the Old rules God gave to

Moses hundreds of years before. AWKWARD.

So then there was an EPICALLY long meeting,

which probably wasn't very INTERESTING,

where everyone just kept saying:

I'm right, you're wrong. End of.

You're wrong, I'm right. That's that.

After HOURS, and HOURS, and HOURS, and

HOURS... everyone was just getting grumpy

and HUNGRY. So Peter told everyone to be quiet
&
and listen.

"Right," he said, CLAPPING his hands. "You all know

that GOD used me to tell the Gentiles about JESUS.

And you all know that God sent the Holy Spirit to fill

the Gentiles, just like he did with you. The Gentiles have

NEVER followed the Old rules — but that doesn't seem to **bother** God, does it!? So why does it bother **YOU**? God doesn't save people just because they follow the rules, it's not like you can **EARN** his love — he saves people because he *loves* them. That's GRACE."

(GRACE? What is **IS** GRACE? Well, it's not just a name, or a **word** that Christians like to sing in church songs — it's actually something **really** important. GRACE is kind of like a super awesome **PRIZE** that you could never be even close to winning — but you get it **anyway**. God shows us GRACE because he *loves* us, even though we could never ever do **enough** to deserve it.)

179

Everyone had definitely stopped talking now. Well, except for Paul and Barney... They **TOLD** everyone, again, about all the **AMAZING** things God had done with the Gentiles. Then James spoke up:

"**LOOK**, we've all heard before from Simon (Peter) that God **loves** the Gentiles, and that's what God **always** said he would do. Don't you remember? God sent **A**mos with a message **hundreds** of years ago saying that he wanted to make a way > for Gentiles to know him, too, and that's **EXACTLY** what he's done. **SO**, I think we should just <u>trust</u> God, and **TRY** to encourage **everyone** who becomes a Jesus follower to live like God would **WANT**. Let's write to them and **HELP** them out. It's not like they **need** us to tell them about all the **RULES** God gave to **Moses** – they can hear those in meeting places **everywhere**."

Sounds like James had got it all sorted to me. (Now) all they needed to do was write their letter – should be **easy**, right?

"Hello, **nice** friendly Gentile Christians in Antioch and round about. Hope you are **well**. We're just writing because Paul and Barney (told) us that some arrogant people came and said some **silly** things to you and made you all confused. So we've picked out a couple of the guys from here to come and hang out with you all. They can tell you **everything** – and especially this: We think the Holy Spirit wants us to **remind** you to live like God would want you to. If you get _that_ right, you'll be just **fine**. See you soon, love from the **J**erusalem apostles."

Who do **YOU** think they chose to deliver the letter?

a) **Paul** and **Barney** ☐

b) **Paul** and **Barney** and **Judas** and **Silas** ☐

c) A pigeon ☐

d) A 7-year-old boy called Ralph ☐

In the end Paul, Barney, Judas and Silas took the letter all the way ◁ back to **ANTIOCH** and when they <u>arrived</u> they got everyone together and read it out. The **Gentiles** in **ANTIOCH** were **SO, SO, SO** happy — they felt much better, and a lot *LESS* **CONFUSED**. Excellent.

Judas and Silas did a **GREAT** job of helping out,

and they were especially good at CHEERING
everyone up. They made SURE everyone was OK
before they went back to Jerusalem. But Paul
and Barney stayed behind and kept on teaching the
Gentiles all about GOD.

A few weeks later Paul was getting
itchy feet. (I mean, not literally, he didn't have a
disease or anything — he just wanted to move on and go
somewhere ELSE) So, he told Barney that they should go
back to all the CITIES and towns they had been to
before and see how the NEW Jesus followers were
getting on. But Barney wanted to bring John — you
remember him? He was the ONE who decided not to

stick with Paul when they were in CYPRUS back in chapter 13. Paul really didn't think that was a good idea, I MEAN, he might just decide to wander off again.

"I'm not coming unless John comes," said Barney with his arms folded. "Well, I'M not having John messing us around again," said Paul with his frowny face.

SO Barney went off with John and got on a boat to Cyprus.

And Paul took Silas WITH him and went off in the other direction, to go and HELP out in the churches in Syria. Epic FALL OUT.

CHAPTER 16

PULLING & YANKING, QUAKING & WAKING...

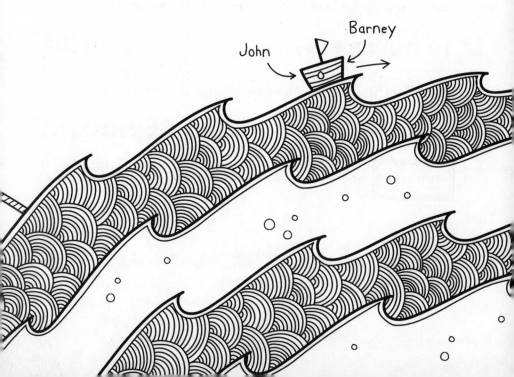

John

Barney

After he'd been back to **S**yria, Paul went back up to

Lystra. And that's where he met **Tim**. Tim was an

INTERESTING guy — he was half Greek and

half Jewish, and he *followed* Jesus. Everyone who knew

♡ ♡ ♡

him loved him. It must be nice to be **that** popular!

Paul decided that Tim would be a **GREAT** guy to work

with, and so he asked him to *JOIN* him on his travels.

But **before** they could leave, Paul had to make **SURE**

that Tim went through some Jewish ceremonies so that

all the Jews they met would take Tim **SERIOUSLY,**

especially when they found out his dad was **GREEK**.

After all that was **sorted**, Paul, Tim and a few others

went from ONE town to the NEXT and told all the people they could find about what the apostles in Jerusalem had decided. They wanted to make SURE that people stayed STRONG in their *faith*, and everywhere they went MORE and MORE people decided to follow Jesus.

The Holy Spirit told them which way to go, which countries they should visit and which ones they should avoid. And one night, Paul had a rather ODD dream. He saw a man from a place called Macedonia standing there in front of him, who just kept on saying, "*PLEASE* come to Macedonia, *PLEASE*!" until eventually Paul woke up and said, "Let's go to Macedonia!" So that's where they went because they knew the dream was from GOD.

And I got to go along TOO! **Anyway**, now it was time for **ANOTHER** boat trip. A *long* one!

It took us **3 WHOLE days** to get to a Roman city in Macedonia called **P**hilippi. We arrived on a Thursday, and on Saturday we decided to **LOOK** for some people to pray with. So we went down for a walk down by the river and **met** a group of women who were there. One of them was called **Lydia**. Lydia loved God, but she hadn't heard about Jesus, so she was **really INTERESTED** in what Paul had to **SAY**. Everyone knew Lydia — she worked in the **CITY** and sold the most *beautiful* purple fabric you can imagine. All soft and smooth, all **PURPLY**

and, well — PURPLE! She didn't know it at the time, but God made her WANT to listen to Paul — he knew she would WANT to follow Jesus when she heard about him, and she did. Lydia and her whole family got baptised and she invited us to come and stay for a while.

A few days later, we were on our way to the river again when we saw a girl who had an evil spirit living inside her. Let's call her Nova. Nova worked for some people who treated her very badly, and used her to make money by telling people their fortunes. As soon as Nova spotted Paul she ran right up to him and then followed all of us everywhere. And I mean everywhere. She kept shouting whenever anyone else came **NEAR**, saying things like:

"These guys are **GOD** slaves, they want to

tell you how to be saved." She was making

everyone stare and **no one** would come near us;

Paul was getting really rather **ANNOYED**. So a

Few days later he just turned round to

her and told the evil spirit to leave. "In the name of Jesus

leave her alone." And it went. Just like that. **DONE**.

SO, if you're Nova, not having the evil spirit any more

was pretty darn **AWESOME**. But if you're

her boss, and suddenly she can't tell fortunes any more and

get you money (because it was the **evil** spirit who was

making her do that), then you might not be **SO** pleased.

190

Nova's bosses were indeed NOT SO pleased, and they grabbed Paul and Silas and took them to the city leaders. "These men are RUINING everything," they said. "They're Jews! And they're telling us to do very Un-Roman things. They're going ROUND upsetting everyone!"

The CROWDS all joined in...

GET RID OF THEM!

THEY'RE TRYING TO RUIN EVERYTHING.

YEAH—HE'S RIGHT!

They all ⋝crushed⋜ in, closer and closer to Paul and Silas, and the leaders didn't even stop them — IN FACT, they egged the crowd on. The closer they got, the smaller the space that Paul and Silas were standing in. They kept ON coming, and then they were PULLING and yanking at all their clothes.

Paul and Silas tried to hold on to their pants, at least, but they even took THOSE! And it didn't get any BETTER...

When they'd taken all their CLOTHES (and I mean ALL their clothes! *eek!*), the city leaders had Paul and Silas ⟹ dragged away and HIT with sticks until they could hardly move, and then thrown in prison with a guard on the door. The guard put them in the deepest part of the prison, and chained their feet to the walls. He was determined they weren't going to escape.

But, GUESS what happened NEXT. Well, I'm sure you haven't *forgotten* what happened when Peter was in prison ! SO maybe it won't be a surprise that...

Paul and Silas didn't sleep AT ALL. They just prayed all the time, and sang lots of JESUS songs. And then the ground shook - really, really shook and there was a super loud CRACK. Every single door in the prison flew wide open, and Paul and Silas' chains just fell on the floor.

Nooooo!

When the guard realised what was going on, and saw all the prisoners coming OUT of their cells, he didn't know what to do. He knew he was going to get in MEGA trouble — and he was thinking of stabbing himself with his OWN sword, before someone else did it, but Paul stopped him.

"**DON'T**!" he **SHOUTED**. "Don't do that! No one has actually escaped! *LOOK* — we're all still here!"

The guard looked around and realised that **everyone** was still there — and they weren't even **trying** to get past him. He looked at Paul and Silas (who still didn't have any clothes — **AWKWARD**!) and knelt down in front of them. He was shaking all over, like a **wobbly** jelly.

"What do I have **to do** to be saved?" he asked Paul. "Can I do it **NOW**?"

"Just *CHOOSE* to *believe* in **JESUS**," replied Paul. "Then you and all of your **FAMILY** will be saved."

194

SO, in the middle of the night, and with **NO** clothes on, Paul and Silas went back to the guard's HOUSE and told him and all his FAMILY about Jesus. The guard sorted out all their CUTS and bruises and gave them something to wear. Then the whole family were baptised, and had a super tasty fish biscuit meal to celebrate!

phew!

YAY

In the morning, the city leaders sent some guards to let Paul and Silas out. So when the guard they were staying with heard this he said: "You should leave. Now is your chance to get out without anyone realising what's happened."

"But they stole our clothes and beat us up. They threw us in prison — and now they want us to conveniently disappear?

NO WAY! If they want us to go away, - they should come and *TELL* us themselves."

When the leaders heard what Paul and Silas were saying they got a LITTLE bit "**scared**", because they'd realised that they were Romans. And beating up Romans was against the LAW — so you wouldn't want to get caught doing that, now, would you? The leaders came out to Paul and Silas and said they were **SORRY**. And told them to go away.

Paul and Silas left Philippi, and on their way out they {popped} back in to see Lydia and her friends and encouraged them to keep on *following* JESUS. Then they carried on with their journey.

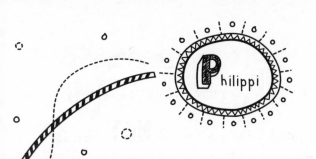

Philippi

CHAPTER 17

THUGGY THESSALONICA

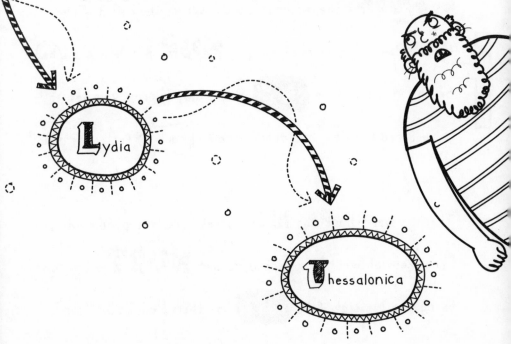

Lydia

Thessalonica

And then things got really rather messy.

Because, you see, Paul and Silas just would **NOT** shut up about JESUS. When they arrived in a place called Thessalonica, they ramped it up — BIG time!

Paul went into the JEWISH meeting place and told everyone there about Jesus. When they said, "The Messiah wasn't supposed to get HURT — how can (he) be the Messiah if he died?" Paul said, "Don't you get it — he suffered for you, and then he came back from the dead!"

Then he went back the **NEXT** week, and the people said, "The Messiah wasn't supposed to get HURT — how <u>can</u> he be the Messiah if he died?" So, then Paul said, "Don't you GET it – he suffered FOR you, and then he came

back ⟹ from the dead!"

And then he went back the NEXT week AGAIN! And

the people said, "The Messiah wasn't supposed to get

HURT – how can he be the Messiah if he died?" So,

then Paul said, "DON'T YOU GET IT – he

suffered FOR YOU, and then he came back ⟹ from

the dead!"

After a while, quite a FEW people were

convinced and decided they wanted to become Jesus followers.

Well – I'm SURE you can imagine that the peeved Jews

weren't so **happy** about that. [IN FACT], they were **SO** unhappy that they went out and found themselves some thugs. Scary looking **THUGS** – the ones that you'd run away > from if you saw them coming **towards** you, the ones with **BIG** frowny eyebrows, a bunch of bruises on their noses and a couple of teeth missing.

"Right, **THUGS**," said the peeved Jews, "we would like you to do your **thuggiest thugging** and go and **THUG** up Paul and Silas! Go, thugs!"

And off they went. The only problem was that these thugs weren't especially **BRIGHT**, and they couldn't find Paul and Silas. Instead, they found **Jason** (he was a **JESUS** *follower*, too) and trashed his house.

Nice.

They **DRAGGED** Jason and his Jesus-following friends by the armpits, all the way back into town, shouting: "These people who are **RUINING** everything — now they've come **here** as well, to **our** town! Jolly Jason and all his **muppet** mates — they're the ones who said these troublemakers could be here. How could they break all our **RULES**?"

They **kept** throwing punches at Jason and his mates.

There were broken noses **everywhere**. Eurgh.

"They **EVEN** say there's another **KING** called Jesus! I mean, seriously — what about the Emperor? He's the (real) king!

Everyone stared at all the broken noses — it was getting a bit awkward. **SO** the town leaders decided to take some cash from these Jesus followers and ⌐tell⌐ them to be on their way.

It seemed like a **GOOD** (idea) for Paul and Silas to maybe *LEAVE* Thessalonica, if they wanted to keep their noses intact. So Jason and his mates sent them **OFF** to a place called **B**erea (say Bare-oh-a), where there would **hopefully** be fewer face-bashing **THUGS**.

The people in **B**erea were actually *pretty* friendly. They listened to what Paul and Silas had to say and really wanted to **FIND OUT** if it was true. When they realised it was indeed all true, loads of them decided to become Jesus followers.

It didn't take *long* for the people in **T**hessalonica to find out what had happened, though. And they were **SERIOUSLY** peeved. So guess what happened next: ???

a) Paul and Silas *RAN* away from **B**erea ☐

b) **T**hessalonica sent their **THUGS** to **B**erea to beat up Paul and Silas ☐

c) **B**erea found some thugs of their **OWN** and sent them → to **T**hessalonica to tell them to leave Paul and Silas alone ☐

d) Paul and Silas dug a **BIG** hole, jumped inside and hoped no one would find them ☐

The Thessolonican THUGS ROCKED up and
started SHOUTING about Paul and Silas,
telling everyone that what they'd heard about this
KING Jesus just wasn't TRUE. But it didn't
work — because all the new Jesus followers managed
to get Paul out of town and send him off to the seaside.
Things weren't SO GOOD for Silas, though... he
stayed behind with Timothy.

Paul eventually got to Athens, and he told the

people who'd **HELPED** him get there to go straight back and get Silas and Timothy, TOO.

While Paul was waiting for Silas and Timothy to come and join him, he got really upset. And it wasn't because he was *lonely*, it was because all the people in Athens were worshipping all the wrong gods. So he went to **ALL** the meeting places and tried to (tell) people about JESUS – but they just weren't getting it.

"What's he ON about?" said one group of {thinkers.} "Can't make out a word he's saying!" "I think he's saying we should believe in some RANDOM *OTHER* gods – why would we do **THAT**?!"

Paul was just explaining that Jesus had died for them and that God loved them, and that Jesus had come back from the DEAD and everything. In the end they took Paul to a big fancy meeting of important leaders called the "Areopagus" (say arry-op-a-gus).

(The Harry stop a bus? NO! The arry-op-a-gus! The Areopagus was a special group of important men who made decisions about the city of Athens. They used to meet on a hill and talk about very important things — like taxes and houses and food and water and stuff.)

"Mr Paul. We would LIKE to understand you," they said. "You seem to be saying some very STRANGE things, and we would like you to *EXPLAIN* what you're

waffling on about." (This is the kind of thing the Areopagus

did **all the time** — they seemed to spend every

day talking about (ideas) and then listening to some more

ideas and talking about those ideas with the first lot of

ideas... **HO HUM** ... Ideas, ideas, ideas...)

I'm not *QUITE* **SURE** they were expecting such

an awesome response from Paul — but this is what they got:

"Hello, Athens people!" said Paul, as he **STOOD UP**

and looked around. "I can tell that you're really bothered

about getting all your **religious** stuff right — you've

got LITTLE statues that you worship all over the place, and

offering tables **everywhere**. I even found one

that had a LITTLE sign on it saying it was for worshipping

an unknown god. How can you worship a god if you don't

know anything about him? I'm talking about a **GOD** that I

DO know. And this is him: he's the God who **MADE**

everything, **YOU** and **ME** included, and he is everywhere.

He doesn't live in a building that people made and he

he doesn't *NEED* people to do anything for him. He has

everything he needs already. He's the (one) who makes

you breathe, he's the one who has been here all along.

He's the (one) who made everything happen just like it has

so far, and he **ABSOLUTELY**, (totally,) completely

and **UTTERLY** loves his people. He desperately

wants them to choose to love him back. People sometimes

think he's **FAR AWAY**, but he's not, he's right here with us all the time. It's like **SOME** of your writers say, 'we come from him'."

Everyone was *listening* to Paul and thinking about what he said, and it was kind of maybe just starting to make **some** sort of *SENSE.*

"**SO**..." Paul continued, "because we come **from** him, he can't be made of a lump of gold, a slab of silver or a punch of pebbles, can he? He can't be some sort of statue that we **MADE.** God let this kind of thing go before, but now he's not going to. He wants you to realise who he **really** is because one day in the future he'll judge

YOU. That's what he said. And it's **TRUE** – you can tell it's true because he **always** does what he says he will. He said he'd bring Jesus ◁back from the dead – and he did!"

A few people started giggling. They thought Paul was a bit silly to say that people can come back from the dead. They figured he was just some CRAZY old man waffling on about ridiculous ideas that didn't make sense – but not everyone thought so. A few people asked Paul if he would come back and talk to them again. And a few others decided to become Jesus followers right then, because of what Paul had told them. Even **ONE** guy from the Areopagus called Dionysius (say Die-on-iss-ee-us) decided to believe, and a woman called Damaris (say Da-mar-iss) did, too.

CHAPTER 18

TIT, CRISP & APOLLOS

After all of that, Paul carried on travelling and went **OFF** to a place called **C**orinth. When he got there he met two people with totally **AWESOME** names — and they were married to each other. **EPIC**.

Aquila (say a-kwil-a) and **P**riscilla (say priss-ill-a) were from **I**taly, but they had ended up in **C**orinth because the Roman guy in charge in **I**taly had made all the Jewish people leave. Nice guy. **Anyhow**, Aquila and Priscilla made tents — and that's what Paul did too! (**COOL** — right?!). So they had **plenty** to talk about straight away — tent materials, tent poles, tent pegs — all things **TENT**, really.

Paul decided he'd STAY with these guys for a while and work for their tent-making company, too. But that didn't MEAN he was going to (stop) talking about Jesus – oh no! Every Saturday he was right there, in the Jewish meeting place, trying to PERSUADE all the people to follow JESUS.

In case you were wondering what had happened to Silas and Tim, they did eventually catch up with Paul, and when they FINALLY arrived Paul decided he was going to do this preaching thing full time.

(What is preaching? You might've heard people (talk) about "preaching" – especially in a church. Sometimes they even call the person doing the "preaching" a "**preacher**".

Well, basically, the word "preach" means "telling people in public", and when Christians (talk) about "preaching" they **really** just mean telling other people about **JESUS** and all the stuff that God says in the Bible. Simples.)

As usual, not everyone was very impressed.

IN FACT, they actually got a bit **NASTY**. (Maybe they'd heard about the **THUGS** in **T**hessalonica...)

But Paul was having <u>none</u> of it. "**RIGHT**. That's **IT**. You've **heard** what I've said — if you don't <u>like it</u>, well, that's up to you. I'm just going to (talk) to the Gentiles now."

And **OFF** he went. Well, he went **NEXT** door anyway

– to **Tit's** HOUSE. (Actually, his <u>real</u> name was Titius Justus, which sounds rather *POSH* to me, so I'm just going to call him Tit.) At Tit's house there was a man called **Crisp.** No seriously – there was! (His <u>real</u> name was Crispus!)

Anyhow. Crisp was a very **IMPORTANT** Jewish leader and when he heard what Paul was saying he decided this Jesus guy was *DEFINITELY* worth *following* – so Crisp and all his **FAMILY** and a whole of load of **other** people from **C**orinth got baptised.

A few days later, Paul was in bed, fast asleep, having an awesome dream about fish biscuits. **SUDDENLY** **GOD** spoke to Paul (while he was <u>still</u> asleep) and said,

"Don't be "scared". Just keep on doing what you're doing. Speak about ME because I am there with YOU. No one is going to get you, no one can HURT you because I've got lots of people working for me in this city."

Paul felt much safer after that, and so he stayed in Corinth for a year and a half and KEPT ON talking about JESUS. And GUESS what? God did exactly what he said he would. He kept Paul safe.

Even when some *PEEVED* Jews managed to kidnap Paul

and take him to court, God **STILL** kept him safe.

When they said: "This man is sneaky. He is trying to

get people to worship **GOD** by doing things that are

against the Law. He's a 'baddun', " God still kept Paul safe.

Paul was about to **DEFEND** himself when the court

leader dude, called Gallio, said, "If you were **ACTUALLY**

complaining about someone who'd done something wrong,

then I'd *listen* to what you were saying, but this doesn't

make **ANY** sense. You're going **on** about this man who

is breaking the law, but it's Jewish Law you're talking about

— it's *NOTHING* to do with me. You sort it out

yourself — I'm not doing it. **GET LOST!**"

But instead of **leaving**, the PEEVED Jews decided to do something to get a **reaction** from this guy — how DARE he say he wasn't going to *listen*!

Before he KNEW it, poor *old* Sosthenes (say soss-ther-nees), one of the Jewish leaders, found himself being PUNCHED in the face and kicked in the ribs, by his (own) people! They kept on beating him up — and **every** time someone smacked him they kept looking at Gallio to see what he'd DO. He didn't do anything. Ouch.

Meanwhile, God still kept Paul safe. For MONTHS, and MONTHS, and MONTHS.

EVENTUALLY, Paul decided it was time to go on another sailing trip, this time back over to **S**yria. And he took **Aquila** and **Priscilla** with him. But, before he left, he did something a bit **ODD** — he shaved off **ALL** his hair. **Every** SINGLE **BIT** of it.

(<u>Why</u> did Paul **CUT** off his hair? Well it **almost** certainly wasn't because he just fancied a **NEW** style, and it was **DEFINITELY** because he'd made a special promise to God saying that he would have all his hair cut off, but I've **NEVER** been able to find out <u>why</u>. <u>Whatever</u> his reasons were, I do know it's **always** good to keep promises you make to **GOD**!)

SO, bald Paul, Aquila and Priscilla sailed off to **S**yria and stopped off at a place called **E**phesus (say Eff-e-suss) on the way. Paul went *OFF* to the Jewish meeting place as **usual** and started *trying* to tell the Jews all about Jesus. They were actually *QUITE* interested in what Paul had to (say) (maybe his new haircut helped?) and asked him to come ◁back◁ another time and carry on talking to them. But Paul said he wouldn't come back unless God (told) him to. And then he got back on the boat and **left.** (Aquila and Priscilla stayed behind to keep on talking about Jesus.)

Paul **ONLY** went where God was telling him, so I (guess) God **must've** told him to go back to **J**erusalem, because that's where he ended up **NEXT.**

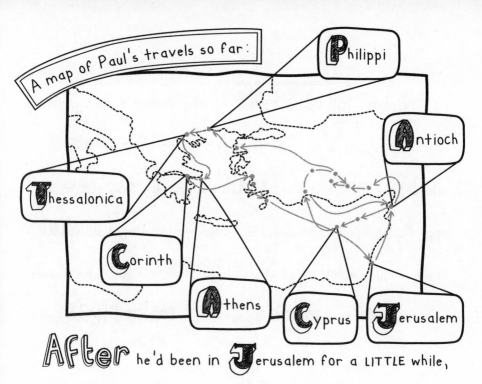

A map of Paul's travels so far:

Philippi

Antioch

Thessalonica

Corinth

Athens

Cyprus

Jerusalem

After he'd been in **J**erusalem for a LITTLE while,

and said "Hi" to the church there, he went off to Antioch

again, and then to a **FEW other** places, so that

he could <u>encourage</u> all the Jesus *followers* in the area.

Back in **E**phesus, a very **CLEVER** nerdy man

called **Apollos** arrived. Apollos really loved God, and

Jesus sounded *pretty* awesome, too. Apollos *KEPT*

talking about JESUS at the Jewish meeting places

???

and asking questions — he just wanted to learn more

and more! Good old Aquila and Priscilla

soon found Apollos, though, and told him all they COULD

about Jesus. Apollos was SO HAPPY to find some people

who could tell him more about this INCREDIBLE guy.

Apollos started travelling around the area and

telling people about Jesus. Because he was SO CLEVER

and knew SO MUCH about God, he managed to prove

to lots of PEEVED Jews that Jesus really was the one

God had sent to save everyone. Even when they tried

to argue with him, Apollos always had something super

AWESOME to say in reply.   o

CHAPTER 19

TISSUES & APRONS

Paul decided it was time to go over to **E**phesus again (obviously, he would've checked with **GOD** first!) and he went on a *long* road through the countryside to get there.

When he **FINALLY** arrived, Paul found some Jesus *followers* and got chatting. He <u>really</u> wanted to know whether or not they were **FILLED** with Holy Spirit, because if they weren't he wanted to pray for them!

(**FILLED** with the Holy Spirit? What's that all about? Well, the ¦Holy Spirit¦ **IS** God. Just like ¦Jesus¦ **IS** God. And just like God the ¦Father¦ **IS** God. Complicated, I know — but *TRUST* me, it's **TRUE**. You remember we talked about the Holy Spirit way back in chapter **2**? Well,

Paul KNEW that God the [Father] wanted **everyone** to have the Holy Spirit living in them, just like he'd [sent →] the Spirit to fill the Jesus followers at Pentecost. But not ALL the NEW Jesus followers KNEW this. Some of them had chosen to *follow* Jesus and love God, and been baptised and **everything**, but hadn't been told about the Holy Spirit...)

Anyway, it turned out a whole lot of these Jesus followers hadn't even **HEARD** about the Holy Spirit — but once they **understood** what Paul was talking about they couldn't wait! Paul explained that they were still JESUS *followers*, and God still loved them, but that God had **even more** to give them.

"LISTEN," said Paul, "when you were baptised that was GREAT, but it was just a baptism that showed you wanted to change, leave your old ways behind and FOLLOW Jesus — let me pray for you now."

And SO Paul put his hands on their heads (not because he thought their heads were "cold", but because it was a good way to pray for them, and for GOD to use Paul as he prayed) and asked the Holy Spirit to come and FILL them up.

The Holy Spirit came and FILLED them from top to toe — and they all spoke in DIFFERENT languages and said ALL kinds of things that God told them to say. WOW!! That was a whole 12 more people who had the Holy Spirit living **inside** of them.

(Living inside of them? **FILLED** with the Spirit? Isn't that a bit creepy? **NO**! Not at all! The Holy Spirit isn't like some sort of creature that lives in your tummy and **wiggles** around. He's **100%** God and **100%** good. I don't **really** know what he's made of, but I know he makes a **BIG** difference — he helps you to **listen** out for God, he helps you to make **GOOD** choices for God, he helps you to be **BRAVE** and know that God is with you and so much more. The Holy Spirit is awesome!)

Paul stayed in **E**phesus for about three months and he did his usual Jewish meeting place speaking **thing**. A few more of the **PEEVED** Jews finally decided to **believe** in what Paul was telling them, but a whole LOAD of others were just plain NASTY.

When the NASTY ones started to say HORRIBLE things about Jesus and Paul, Paul didn't hang around. He went OFF with the NEW Jesus followers to a place down the road. Paul kept on doing this for a whole 2 years — just talking and talking about Jesus — and you know, he never <u>once</u> got bored. He loved Jesus SO MUCH — he knew that God had sent Jesus to save everyone and he just couldn't stop talking about it.

God did AMAZING things through Paul — he healed people; he got RID of evil spirits. IN FACT , some

228

people even brought tissues to see Paul. Yes,

I did say tissues. Well, handkerchiefs anyway. And aprons.

SO, I know this sounds a bit STRANGE,

well more than a bit strange, actually — but they brought

their handkerchiefs and aprons, so that Paul could send

them back with prayers attached. It wasn't that he

prayed for the handkerchiefs and aprons, it was that

God saw how much faith people had and so he gave them

GOOD things. After ALL, people were only coming to

Paul because they believed God was working through him,

and so what did it MATTER if he worked through

their handkerchiefs and aprons too?! Whenever a handkerchief

or apron had been touched by Paul (but really, by

GOD in Paul) it helped to **HEAL** people who were poorly when they touched it. Woah. That's kind of awesome.

A **FEW** of the local Jews who **weren't** Jesus followers had also started trying to get rid of **evil** spirits and **HEAL** people. They decided the BEST way to do it would be to pray for people, and use Jesus' name in their prayers — *I MEAN*, that seemed to work for Paul — right?

WELL, it didn't work for them. **BIG** time. One day, they had just told this **evil** spirit to go away when it said, "Now I know who JESUS is, and I know who Paul is, but who do you {think} you are?" And then it *ATTACKED* them through the man it was living inside. IN FACT , it stole their clothes so they

had to RUN away wearing absolutely nothing and

covered in cuts and bruises. Ouch.

When people 𝕩𝕩𝕩𝕩𝕩𝕩 heard what had happened they were

SERIOUSLY FREAKED out. Clearly, this

Jesus guy wasn't someone to be messed with — there was

real ⟨power⟩ in his name, you couldn't just SAY it and

not really mean it. You couldn't just pretend to

follow Jesus and hope for the best — he was the real deal.

People came to the meeting places and put all their books

about trying to heal people with magic on a GIANT

bonfire. There were SO MANY books that if you'd

tried to buy them all it would have cost THOUSANDS of pounds. That's one BIG bonfire. Slowly but SURELY, people began to hear about Jesus and all that he said and did, and more and more began to believe.

Paul decided it was time to go ← back to Jerusalem and then take a SUPER long journey to Rome.

But not **everyone** in **E**phesus was HAPPY about everything that Paul had done. Especially when it meant they couldn't *EARN* as much **money** as they were doing before **Paul** had arrived.

There was this one guy called **Dem** who used to make statues of Greek gods out of ⟨SILVER⟩ - well, of **ONE** Greek god in particular, called ⟨Artemis.⟩ Before Paul **showed** up, he used to sell loads of them and made himself quite a *nice* pile of cash — and now he **hardly** sold **anything**.

He got his ⟨SILVER⟩-making mates **together** and ⟨told⟩ them all that it was Paul's *FAULT* that they couldn't make their **money** any more.

"This Paul **DUDE**, he's the one who *RUINED* this for us. He's the one who has told **everyone** far and wide that god statues aren't really gods - at all. - Of course, it's not just **US** that loses out — what about these **GREEK** gods that we're *trying* to keep happy? What about ⟨Artemis?⟩ People won't love her any more. I **mean** — that'd be terrible, wouldn't it...?"

Dem managed to get **everyone MAD**. <u>Very</u> **MAD**. So **MAD**, ⟨IN FACT⟩, that they started **SHOUTING** about how great all their LITTLE **SILVER** gods were, and running around trying to catch anyone who was known

234

for hanging out with Paul. They found a FEW of Paul's

mates and ≡dragged them into the meeting place. When

Paul FOUND out — he wanted to go there himself and

sort everything out, but the other Jesus followers

told him he really couldn't come over — it was JUST

too dangerous.

LOADS and LOADS of people were there in the
CROWD and they were all SHOUTING at the

tops of their voices. It must've been super LOUD and

super "SCARY" — they weren't even all SHOUTING

the same thing. They were really CONFUSED — some

of them didn't even know (why) there were there, they'd

just followed the crowds!

ER...WHY
AM I HERE

Eventually, they PUSHED a guy called Alex into the →middle← of the stage in front of the crowds and told him to explain himself. Alex didn't know WHAT to do — he waved his arms around a lot and tried to get everyone to shut up. Everyone started to quiet down a LITTLE bit, when SUDDENLY someone shouted, "Hey! He's a Jew!!" And that was the end of Alex's chance — because when they realised he wasn't even Greek, they decided he couldn't POSSIBLY be allowed to say anything about their Greek gods, so they JUST shouted, constantly, for 2 hours.

"Our GREEK GODS ROCK! Great is Artemis! Great is Artemis!" — just imagine hearing that for two hours in a ROW!

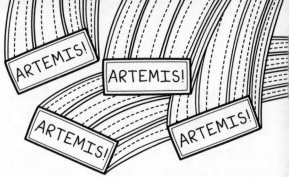

FINALLY, one of the city leaders managed to get them all to (stop) shouting. "Calm down, you lot!" he said, while waving his arms like a chicken. "**Everyone** knows Ephesus is the place where we look after the great Artemis. You've *DRAGGED* these people in here and they haven't done anything wrong at all. Did they go and trash the **GREEK** temple? Did they **RUIN** all your statues? Did they say your Greek gods were **evil**? (No!) If you have **real** problem with them, or you can actually say what they did wrong, then come to the court house and tell **everyone** and we'll have a **PROPER** trial. Now, if you don't all chill out and

237

go home we'll all get arrested for causing chaos for **NO** reason — is that what you <u>want</u>?"

After that, everyone went home **muttering** under their breath about Paul and his mates. They'd have to think of a BETTER way to get their own back...

CHAPTER 20

PO-TAY-TER, ITCHY-BUS & LOTS OF TEARS

After **everything** had calmed down, Paul managed

to get everyone back→together←and say "good bye" before

he went OFF on his travels.

He made LOTS of stops on his way and encouraged all

the JESUS followers he could find to keep

going and stay STRONG. But he didn't stay for very

long in one place because he knew he had to keep on

travelling to find MORE people to (tell) about Jesus.

He was about to get on a boat to Syria when he heard

that there was a plot to HURT him — and the plotters

were waiting on the boat. WOW — that was

close! So Paul didn't get on that boat and went back to

some of the towns inland *INSTEAD.*

Paul took a whole **LOAD** of Jesus-following friends with him — and they all had **FABULOUS** names! There was **Sopater** (rhymes with PO-TAY-TER), **Aristarchus** (rhymes with A-FIST-SHARK-BUS), **Secundus** (rhymes with THE-FUN-BUS), **Gaius** (rhymes with DAY-BUS), **Tim** (well, that's an easy one) and **Tychicus** (rhymes with ITCHY-BUS)! Oh → — and there was **me** as well!

This awesomely named **CREW** set off before Paul, to a place called **Troas**, to make sure **everything** was **OK**, and we caught them up five days **later**. And

241

then it was time for some truly EPIC stuff!

On Sunday evening we were hanging out TOGETHER in a BIG upstairs room, remembering the last meal Jesus had with his mates before he died. Paul talked and talked about Jesus, and he kept on talking until midnight — and everyone kept on listening, to every single word. Well, almost everyone.

Even though they had all the LIGHTS on, one guy just couldn't keep his eyes open. He was SOOOOOO sleepy. And for a sleepy guy, he hadn't exactly sat in

242

a **SENSIBLE** place... He was all CURLED up on the window ledge, trying to hold his eyes open with his fingers, but it just wasn't working. He *finally* nodded off and FELL out the window — and that was the end of him. AWKWARD.

ONLY, it wasn't quite the end — because when Paul realised what had happened he went outside to find the guy and scooped him up OFF the floor.

"Don't worry!" said Paul, "he's not **DEAD** — he's alive!"

Everyone laughed awkwardly. HA. HA. HA. The guy had just fallen out of the window and landed with a SPLAT on the ground.

243

He clearly wasn't ALIVE. He looked pretty dead to me!

Anyhow, Paul carried the "alive" man inside, then he went on talking about Jesus until the morning — when he decided it was time to GO.

When the people left behind went in to see the sleeping window-falling guy, he was alive and well, so they took him home — totally AMAZED. (Now — I should just say that definitely doesn't mean you should try jumping out of windows and just HOPING it'll all be all right in the morning!)

The NEXT day, we got on a boat to a place called Assos,

244

but **Paul** didn't come with us. He'd decided to meet us in **A**ssos *AFTER* he'd walked all the way there.

Anyway, a long walk and **4** boat trips LATER we all arrived TOGETHER in a place called **M**iletus. While we were **there**, Paul sent a message to the leaders of the church in **E**phesus asking them to come over and visit us — which they **DID**.

When they arrived, Paul told them **everything** that had *HAPPENED* to him.

"You know how MUCH I love Jesus, don't you? You know that I've done **everything** I possibly could for him

while I've been in this area. I've done **everything GOD** told me to do, even when some of the Jews tried to make it **really** hard for me. But they didn't put me OFF. I've told you **everything** I could about Jesus — **everything** that I {thought} might **HELP** you. I've travelled all over the place and told **JEWS, GREEKS, everyone** I could find that God loves them and wants them to turn back to him and **follow** Jesus. And now, I'm going back to Jerusalem and I don't know what's going to **happen** to me. I know that's where God wants me to go — the Holy Spirit told me, but he (also) told me that it was going to be tough. He said I'd end up in prison again, and that there'd be SO many people who were against me. But I KNOW that God is WITH me – and my life isn't the important thing, it's doing what GOD wants, finishing the race HE'S started, telling everyone I possibly can about how GREAT and awesome and WONDERFUL and kind and AMAZING he really, really is."

This was a SUPER passionate speech. Paul looked all happy and sad, chilled out and proper scared – all at the same time. But he STILL had more to say:

"You're not going to see me again. NOT EVER. And that's WHY I asked you to come and see me today – to make sure that everything is as it should be between us. I've only ever told you everything that GOD wants. But now it's over to YOU. Look after everyone – rely on the Holy Spirit to help you. God has given you a CHURCH of people to look after, people that he loves and died for. You're like shepherds looking after sheep. And when I've GONE things are going to get harder. There'll be people who turn against you and try to make things HARD. They'll be like angry wolves trying to eat your sheep – EVEN some of the people in your church – they'll turn against you and TRY to take people away from Jesus, so be BRAVE. Be STRONG! Don't forget that I warned you."

Paul was crying now. Tears were **rolling** down his face as he looked the church leaders in the eye and prayed for them. It was making **ME** *pretty* tearful, **TOO,** I <u>have</u> to say.

"I'm giving **YOU** to God. You look after them now, **GOD**, give them what they *NEED*, keep them close to you. You know I have **NEVER** wanted what others have, I have **ONLY** ever taken what **I** needed and what those ←around→ me needed. I've **always** shown **everyone** how important it is that we look after people with less than us, just like **JESUS** did. He

249

told us that it was BETTER to be a GIVER than to be someone who is given TO."

And then Paul was on his KNEES, sobbing. Everyone knelt down around him, and they were crying, too. They hugged him and tried to help him up. They were all SO SAD and they just couldn't believe they were NEVER going to see Paul again. In the end, they walked with Paul to the boat and watched him get on board.

Sad. Really sad. I've got tears in my eyes just remembering it.

CHAPTER 21

TYRES, CHAINS
& HEAD SHAVING

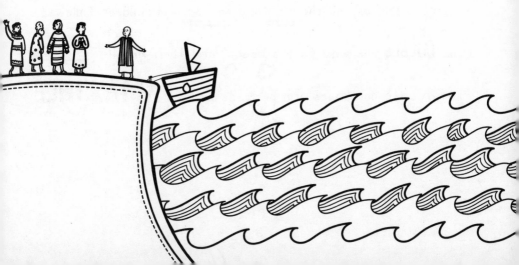

And so the journey BEGAN. It was a *long* one, too.

When we got to a place called Tyre (not the car kind!) we got off the boat For a while and took a week-long break. We managed to find a bunch of Jesus followers to stay with, and they kept on telling Paul that going to Jerusalem really wasn't a good idea, — but they didn't manage to change his mind.

When it was time to go back to the boat, everyone came (with) us. All the men and women and children followed us ALL the way to the beach, and then we all *FELL* down onto our knees and prayed. It was AMAZING!

Our **NEXT** stop was in a place called **P**tolemais (say Per-toll-er-may-iss) where we stayed with some more **JESUS** *followers*. Then, in the morning, we got back on the boat and went to a place called **C**aesarea — where **Philip** lived. (You remember Philip, right? He's the one that **GOD** picked up from a pond where he'd baptised the man in the chariot and then plonked him down somewhere **else**... check out chapter 8 again if you've **FORGOTTEN**.)

Philip's daughters were **AMAZING**. God used them **ALL** to be his messengers and tell people what he was saying! **WOW**! Anyway — after we'd been with Philip for a few days **another GOD** messenger turned up. His name was Agabus (what an AWESOME name!) and he had a message for Paul. Only he didn't just "say" his message, if you know what I mean — he "did" it!

So, we're all STOOD there and Agabus just comes over to Paul and starts to undress him — erm... WHAT?

Thankfully, he stopped when he'd taken off Paul's belt — but then he started tying himself up with the belt. He tied his own hands and feet together so he couldn't ←move→ (and to be honest, he looked a bit WEIRD!), and then he said something really, really SCARY.

"The Holy Spirit told me to come here and do this — because this is what's going to happen to Paul. This is what the

Jews are going to do to him when they CATCH him; then they're going to DELIVER > him to the Gentiles."

SUDDENLY it wasn't QUITE so funny that Agabus was sat there with Paul's belt round his arms and legs — it was terrifying. [Surely] Paul couldn't be serious about going to Jerusalem — it was so obvious bad things were going to happen!

We tried everything we could {think} of to stop !!! Paul from going.

PLEASE, PAUL — WE NEED YOU!

IT'S NOT SAFE, PAUL, CAN'T YOU SEE?

PAUL, DON'T GO!

CAN'T YOU JUST STAY HERE?

In the end, we were ALL in tears and just begging Paul not to go, but he said: "Why are you crying? PLEASE don't — you're breaking my heart. I have to go where GOD [sends] me. I'm ready for this — not just being tied up, but I'm ready to give my life for Jesus."

There was nothing more WE could do, it was up to God now.

◇ ▽ ◇ ▽ ◉ ▽ ◇ ▽ ◇ ▽ ◉ ▽ ◇ ▽ ◇ ▽ ◉ ▽ ◇ ▽ ◇

SO, we started our journey to Jerusalem. No one really knew WHAT to say to each other, everyone was so quiet. A FEW people from Caesarea came with us and HELPED us find places to stay with some of the other Jesus followers they knew along the way.

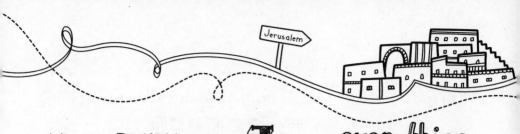

When we FINALLY got to Jerusalem everything started off pretty well — all the Jesus followers there were really ✿ nice to us. When Paul went to SEE James and some of the OTHER church leaders and told them about everything that had happened with the Gentiles, they were SOOOOOOO happy.

"Paul!" they said, "this is so, so WONDERFUL." But then their smiles faded away and they patted Paul on the shoulder, saying, "We do have a TINCY, wincy problem, though. LOADS of Jewish people have decided to follow Jesus, too, which is GREAT, but they still really care about all the Jewish laws.

257

People have *TOLD* them that when you've been talking to Jews and Gentiles **TOGETHER** you've told **everyone** that the old Jewish laws don't **really** matter any more. We don't **really** know what to (do) — because when they **FIND OUT** you're <u>here</u>, well, things might get a bit tricky. But it's **OK** — don't worry, we've got a PLAN."

It was an **INTERESTING** plan, and I was **really** hoping it might sort **everything** out...

"We have found four Jewish men who have made promises to **GOD** — they're going to shave all their hair off as a **SIGN** to God that they're *following* him.

If you go WITH them, and get all your hair shaved too, and pay for everything, then everyone will know you're just the same as the normal rule-following Jews. And we've sent a letter to all the Gentile Jesus followers and told them which RULES to follow, TOO, so that should be fine."

So that's what Paul did. He went OFF with these four guys and shaved all his hair off (again!). They had to stay TOGETHER in the TEMPLE for a while and make sure they did everything PROPERLY. After 7 days it would be official — they would have made their SPECIAL commitment to GOD and everyone would know it.

It was all going pretty well, and we were all praying this would be the end of all the hassle, but then some Jews who'd come to Jerusalem from places Paul had visited on his travels turned up. They recognised Paul STRAIGHT away and started 'shouting' about him.

"It's HIM! It's that man! HE'S the one who told everyone our rules don't matter! Look, he's even brought a Greek man into our Jewish Temple – how can it be SPECIAL any more now HE'S been allowed inside?!" The crowds had seen Paul with a Greek guy in the city, and they figured HE must've been in the Temple TOO... but they were wrong – that didn't seem to bother them too much, though.

260

They were **SHOUTING** pretty loudly, and

people kept sticking their heads out of their windows to

SEE what was going on. People poured out of

their HOUSES and seemed to appear from

every street, and they were chasing Paul.

To be HONEST, Paul didn't stand a <u>chance</u>. There were

thousands of them and only ONE of him, and they soon

managed to grab him. They YANKED him away and

SLAMMED the gates of the Temple firmly closed.

This was IT. They were trying to finish him off. They

were kicking and punching him. Spitting in his FACE,

screaming horrible things at him and pulling at all

his clothes. I could **hardly** watch.

But **SUDDENLY** they stopped and it all went *QUIET.*

They were all staring at something, but I couldn't quite

see **WHAT**. The Romans had arrived! Someone had told

one of the leaders of the Roman army that there was

something **BIG** happening in **J**erusalem, and so

he'd come **straight** over with a bunch of his soldiers.

"**RIGHT**, you lot," he **SHOUTED**. "Get out of the

way. Soldiers — grab him and chain him up."

They chained Paul up with **2** massive chains and *DRAGGED*

him away. The army leader asked the crowd what Paul had

done, and **why** they'd been beating him up — but he couldn't **figure** out what they were saying because **everyone** was speaking at once and just shouting **RIDICULOUS** things. In the **end**, he gave up and told the soldiers to lock Paul in prison. But even that wasn't easy — the crowd ran after the soldiers as they **DRAGGED** Paul along and **kept on** trying to kick and punch him. The soldiers had to carry Paul above their heads just so the **CROWDS** couldn't get to him. They **kept on YELLING**:

Take him away!

Kill him!

We don't want this man in **our** city!

As they got to the prison door, Paul **SHOUTED** to the army leader. "Can I ask you something?"

"You can speak **Greek?**" the army leader said — slightly

surprised that such a **dodgy**-looking prisoner spoke so

well... "<u>You're</u> that guy who took a load of freedom fighters

out into the desert months and months ago, aren't you?"

"**NO**, I'm not," said Paul. "I'm Jewish, from the city of

Tarsus. *PLEASE* — I just want to speak to the people."

The army leader told the soldiers to put Paul **down**

so that he could stand on the steps outside the prison,

and when he was standing he waved his arms around

and **everyone** went quiet. [IN FACT], they went

so quiet you could've heard someone s n e e z e.

And then he **SPOKE.**

CHAPTER 22

PAUL SAYS IT ALL

"Please, hear me out." And **everyone** stayed silent.

Paul was speaking in **Aramaic** — and that made the **CROWDS** listen up.

(What is **Aramaic**? Well, Aramaic is a language — a very **old** one that came from a group of languages including **Hebrew**. Paul could speak Greek **AND** Aramaic, and switched between the two *QUITE* easily. **MOST** of the people in the crowds would've understood Aramaic — it was **kind of** like their local language — so they would've been **INTERESTED** to hear Paul speak in a language that was "normal" to them.)

"I'm Jewish, just like YOU. I was born in Tarsus, but I grew up (here) in Jerusalem, just like so many of you. I was taught about the rules we follow, by a BRILLIANT teacher. I learned about the story of our people, just like YOU have. I love God just as much as any of you. I was the one who had loads of those JESUS followers killed; I was the one who said they'd got it all wrong and wanted to get RID of them. The priests will tell you what I did — they know! I even got letters from Jewish leader people in Jerusalem so that I could go to other cities and say that these Jesus followers needed slinging in jail and beating up, and preferably getting RID of for ever! But THEN it all CHANGED for me..."

Paul spoke with **TEARS** in his eyes — he desperately wanted the **CROWDS** to understand what he was telling them — he wanted them to KNOW Jesus for themselves.

"I was walking on the road to **D**amascus when there was this ridiculously "scary", bright white light that made me fall over, and then I heard the voice of **JESUS**. Jesus was speaking to ME- **Paul** — the Jesus follower killer! He said, 'Saul, why do you **HATE** me so much? Why are you trying to *hurt* me?' When I asked him who he was, he said he was Jesus — **WOAH**!

"**Everyone** with me saw that "scary" light, too

– but they didn't hear the **voice**. I asked Jesus what

he wanted me to do, and he *TOLD* me to go down the

road into town and I'd find out what the **PLAN** was.

Only, I couldn't see – the light was *SO* bright it had

hurt my eyes, so my mates had to hold my hand and help

me into town so I didn't *FALL OVER* or anything!"

Paul was speaking quickly, trying to include **everything**

that had happened, trying to **HELP** people (see) that

GOD really had changed him and shown him the truth.

"When we got into town, God [sent] a guy called **Ana**

to visit me, and he prayed for me and then I could **SEE**.

He told me that God had chosen me to do **AMAZING**

things and that he wanted me to tell as MANY other

people as POSSIBLE about him. So that's what I've

been doing — right from that moment I got up, got

baptised and started telling everyone I could find

the GOOD NEWS about Jesus. When I got back

to Jerusalem, God told me that I needed to go somewhere

else because people here wouldn't listen to what I had

to say. I told him that I was prepared to do anything

for him — that I was the (one) who had tried to get RID

of the Jesus followers, that I was the (one) who watched

people throw rocks at Steve until he was dead. But

God told me to go far away, and he sent me to the Gentiles."

Everyone had actually been doing a pretty good

job of *listening* to Paul until he said "Gentiles". Then it all went rather **wrong**. They started shouting again, screaming LOUDER and LOUDER: "Take him away! Get RID of him! We don't want him! He doesn't deserve to stay alive!" The crowds starting stamping their feet and chanting, "We **HATE** Paul. We **HATE** Paul. We **HATE** Paul!" And then they starting spinning their cloaks around and making mini dust storms. It was completely MAD!

The Romans took Paul inside and got ready to do awful things to him. They were going to tie him to a BIG pillar and hit him on the back with a long spiky whip until he answered their questions. Ewwwww...

271

But just BEFORE they got started Paul said: "Are

you SURE you can hit a Roman man who hasn't even

done anything wrong?"

With their spiky whips in mid-air, the soldiers SUDDENLY

stopped and looked at each other with super "scared"

faces. They went to Claud (he was the officer in charge)

and said, "This guy says he's a ROMAN — what are

we supposed to do now?" So Claud went to ask Paul

if this was true, and when he heard that it was he was

SERIOUSLY worried. He sent away the men

with spiky whips — he knew he'd get into some major

sort of trouble if the Roman leaders found out he'd put a

Roman man in prison.

In the **morning**, he let Paul out of jail, but he still

wanted to find out <u>exactly</u> why all these Jews were so mad.

So, Claud gathered together all of the **IMPORTANT**

Jewish leaders and got them all to wait for a **while**.

Then he brought **Paul** in and started a proper trial.

CHAPTER 23

GARY, UNCLE PAUL & DODGY FELIX

So Paul STOOD there, in front of all the important

Jewish leaders, and told them that he had ONLY done

what GOD had asked of him. That didn't go down very

well. IN FACT , the religious leader in charge told everyone

near Paul to punch him in the mouth so that he wouldn't

be able to keep on telling lies. And they did. Ouch.

But Paul kept on talking: "God will GET you —

God can see what's underneath your posh clothes and your

RULE following — he knows what's in your hearts.

Look at you — telling me I'm breaking the rules, but you're

breaking your OWN rules by telling people to HIT me!"

"You can't say that to the leader, the one that God

has chosen to LEAD us!"

"Well, I'm **sorry**, I didn't realise he was the leader," said Paul, "but what I said is STILL TRUE."

When Paul looked at them all standing there GLARING at him, he realised that there were two **DIFFERENT** groups of JEWS in the CROWD – some who believed in life after death and some who didn't. He knew exactly what he needed to say.

"Listen to me – I'm here because I believe that the dead can come BACK to life because of GOD."

Well, let me tell **YOU**, that was like throwing a cat into a room full of pigeons. People started **SHOUTING** and yelling, and some were actually throwing punches at each other — those who **agreed** that God could bring people back from the dead kept saying that Paul should be released and those who **disagreed** just got angrier and angrier.

"He hasn't done **anything** wrong — maybe God really *DID* speak to him!" said the people who agreed with Paul. "No — he's **BREAKING** all the *RULES,* God would never make him do that!" said the others.

When the **CROWDS** managed to get to Paul they started *PULLING* him, yanking at his arms — and

278

Claud was *worried* they might tear him in HALF if he let them carry on. So he sent in his soldiers to rescue Paul and take him back to prison.

I *suppose* you're probably getting used to what happens when Paul is in prison — GOD shows up! But that doesn't make it any *LESS* AWESOME — and when he showed up this time, he told Paul that he needed to be BRAVE, and that, just like he'd sent him to Jerusalem to tell *everyone* about him, soon he'd be sending him to Rome, too.

Meanwhile, the peeved Jews were getting more and more peeved — these Romans seemed to be protecting

Paul, not helping them get *RID* of him! So they decided to

hatch a **SNEAKY** plan. A **SNEAKY**,

"tummy-rumbling" plan.

There were **40** of them who had decided they were going

to get rid of Paul **once** and for **all**– and that they

weren't going to eat or drink **anything** until they'd

>killed< him. They even went and told the Jewish leaders

that they'd made this sneaky plan and asked them to help!

"**OK**. So here's what you need to do," they said. "Tell the

Roman army leader that you want him to bring Paul back

so that you can ask him some more questions — and then

we'll catch him and **FINISH** him off before he gets

to you." WOW. Just WOW! I can't believe the Jewish leaders were happy to do something so awful. But even with such a SNEAKY plot that involved SO many people, there were still some people who wanted to protect Paul — including his sister's son! I can't QUITE remember his name — let's call him Gary for now.

Gary liked to hang around in the Jewish meeting places — he often HID behind doors and walls, just so he could hear what all the IMPORTANT men were talking about. But when he heard what they were PLANNING to do to Uncle Paul, he knew he had to do something.

He RAN all the way to the army prison without

stopping and BURST through the gates. He RAN down every corridor until he found Uncle Paul and reported what he'd heard. Paul told one of the soldiers guarding him to take Gary to SEE Claud.

Holding Gary by the EAR, owch! the soldier took him to Claud and said, "Paul told me to bring THIS gentleman to you, because he has something he wants to say to you."

"PLEASE, Mr Roman army man, sir, I heard what the Jews said they were going to do to Uncle Paul. They SAID they're going to (tell) you to bring him to the meeting place TOMORROW so they can ask him more

??? questions — but they're going to KILL him before he

even gets there!

You've got to DO something! PLEASE, Mr Roman

army man! They said they weren't going to eat or drink

anything until they'd got RID of him! They're just

waiting for you to take Uncle Paul over there!"

Claud told Gary not to tell anyone else about the

SNEAKY plan, and then he decided he would have

to make a plan of his OWN to keep Paul safe.

He spoke with two of his BEST soldiers and told them

to get together 200 men who could fight by hand,

another 70 men who could fight on horses and another 200 men with spears. "Take all these soldiers, and Paul, and go to Caesarea after 9pm tonight. Make sure that Paul has a horse, TOO, and take him straight to Felix."

470 soldiers, 70 horses and 200 spears! Claud was obviously *pretty* serious about making sure Paul was OK! **Anyway**, while all the soldiers were getting ready, Claud wrote a letter to Felix.

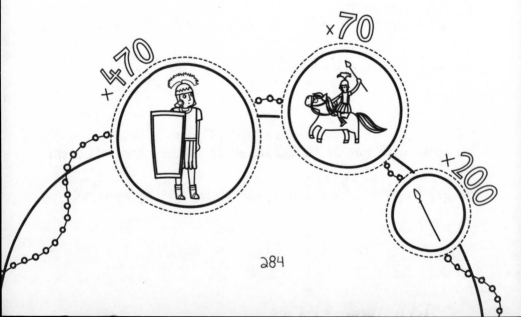

FACT FILE

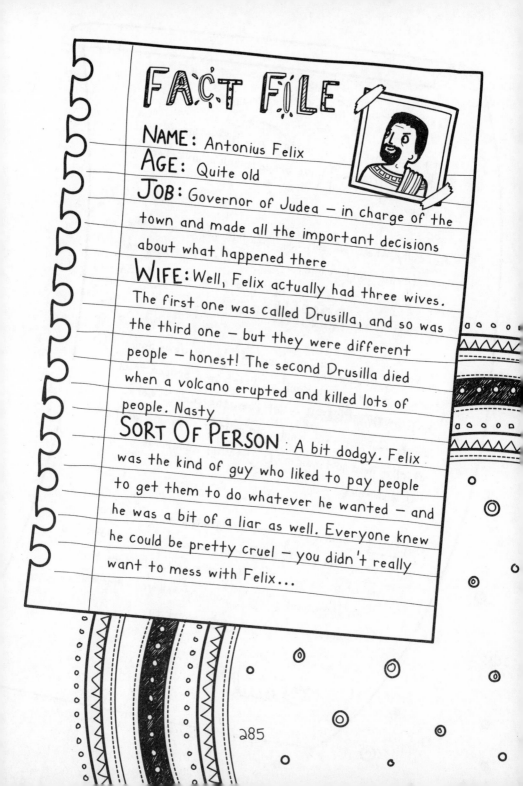

NAME: Antonius Felix

AGE: Quite old

JOB: Governor of Judea — in charge of the town and made all the important decisions about what happened there

WIFE: Well, Felix actually had three wives. The first one was called Drusilla, and so was the third one — but they were different people — honest! The second Drusilla died when a volcano erupted and killed lots of people. Nasty

SORT OF PERSON: A bit dodgy. Felix was the kind of guy who liked to pay people to get them to do whatever he wanted — and he was a bit of a liar as well. Everyone knew he could be pretty cruel — you didn't really want to mess with Felix...

Dear Wonderful Amazingly Fabulous Felix,

It's Claud here, I'm sending this letter to explain **why** my soldiers have brought this man called Paul to you.

Basically, the Jews don't *LIKE* him very much. They were trying to kill him, but my soldiers managed to save him — which is a good job, because then I found out that he's a ROMAN citizen!

I was determined to find out **why** the Jews had such a problem with Paul, so I set up a proper trial and **everything** — but even that didn't work. It turned out that Paul hadn't done anything wrong at all — he'd just said a (few) things about the Jewish rules.

Then I heard the Jews were planning to kill him anyway, no **matter** what I said, so I decided I'd send him to you. I've told the Jewish leaders they can come and SEE you and tell you what their issues are, if they really want to.

Cheers,

Claud

SO Paul and his hundreds of soldiers *SET OFF* in the **night** and got about halfway to **C**aesarea before they needed a rest. In the **morning**, the soldiers on horses kept going **WITH** Paul, while all the others went ⟨back⟩ home.

When they arrived, they gave Paul and the letter about him to **Felix**. Paul **STOOD** there while Felix peered at the letter from Claud. Felix kept looking up at Paul and squinting at him with a slightly **WONKY** frown.

EVENTUALLY, Felix said, "Where are you from?"

"**T**arsus," said Paul. That answer seemed to make Felix think, because he said he'd **wait** until the peeved Jews arrived to **explain** what was going on before he did

anything with Paul.

In the meantime, Felix found Paul a

rather **nice** palace (with dungeons, obviously) to stay

in — and he still had guards making SURE he didn't

do a runner!

CHAPTER 24

MOST LOVELIEST
FABULOUS FELIX

It took a whole 5 days for the PEEVED Jews to arrive in Caesarea, and they even brought a law expert with them. They told Felix that Paul was always causing trouble, that he was always trying to divide people up and make them fight with each other, that he had a secret group of followers and that he said all KINDS of things that really upset people.

But they made SURE they buttered up Felix good and proper first.

"Oh, most MARVELLOUS, wonderful and fabulous Felix," they swooned. "We think you're an AMAZING leader, you've done such a GOOD job running our area, and we think it's truly WONDERFUL that you've

taken a few minutes to hear a TINY complaint. We don't

want to tire you out, we'll just very quickly explain what's

been happening. Thank you so much, most loveliest Felix."

And THEN they said all their NASTY stuff about

Paul, ending with:

"See for YOURSELF, fabulous Felix. He's a troublemaker."

Felix LOOKED at Paul and waved his hand — telling Paul

it was time for him to SAY something.

"I know you've been a leader here for a long time

Felix — so I'm QUITE happy to tell you what's been going on. You know it's <u>true</u> that less than two weeks ago I went to Jerusalem to worship GOD, and I didn't do any arguing in the meeting places there. I didn't talk to any BIG crowds or anything like that. They can't say I did any of those things — because I didn't. Yes, it's TRUE that I worship GOD and I'm a Jesus follower — and they think that Jesus followers are some sort of <u>dodgy</u> group who believe STRANGE things, but they're wrong. I believe everything that <u>they</u> believe — I believe in all the rules <u>they</u> believe in, and I love God just as much as <u>they</u> do. I know that in the END it will ALL be up to GOD — so I always TRY to do what he would want."

Felix nodded and told the *PEEVED* Jews to keep
ssshh!
quiet. He encouraged Paul to carry on.

"I'd been away for years and years, but I came

back to Jerusalem to worship GOD. When these men

found me I was at the Jewish Temple, with my head shaved,

making my PROMISES to God. I wasn't in a

CROWD and I wasn't doing anything except minding

my (own) business. I know there are some Jews I met on

my travels who really didn't like the things I said

— maybe they should be here telling you what I've done.

But THESE men, maybe they should actually say what

it is I've DONE. What was it they said against me

when I stood before them all in Jerusalem? The only

293

thing I said when I was there was that I **believed** God could bring the ~~dead~~ back to life — maybe it was that...''

Felix may not have been the most HONEST man, but he certainly wasn't stupid, and he'd heard a LOT about these JESUS followers. So he told the peeved !!!! Jews to go away and come back when he asked for them.

''I'm going to send for Claud to come here <u>himself</u> and tell me what's going on. THEN I'll decide what to do with Paul,'' he said. Felix sent Paul ◁back▷ to his rather *nice* palace prison and told the guards they could let in a few visitors sometimes and let Paul out every now and again, but that they should still keep an EYE on

him — just in case he tried **anything**.

WELL, I don't think Paul was expecting Felix and his wife to send for him, but they **DID**... They wanted to hear Paul (talk) about Jesus. Paul told them about how wonderful Jesus is and he told them how Jesus wants people who follow him to live **DIFFERENTLY** — to live like God wants them to — doing things how God wants them done — and that ultimately God would be the one to judge them all in the end.

When he got to the bit about JUDGEMENT, Felix **SUDDENLY** decided he'd had enough — he was scared, — he KNEW he didn't live like God would want him to — and he told Paul to **leave** — right away!

295

"Er... Thank you **very much**, Paul. That was just 'great'. I'll let you know when we can chat again. **OK**. You can **GO** now!" he said as he hurried Paul out of the room.

Felix **KEPT** sending for Paul to come and chat with him. Really, he was hoping that Paul might **TRY** and give him a pile of money as a way of getting him to let him out of prison, but he didn't — Paul never <u>once</u> gave Felix any money.

This went on for **AGES**. **2** years, actually, until a guy called **Festus** took over from **Felix**. Festus didn't even know who Paul **WAS**, so Felix could've let Paul **GO**, but he decided he'd rather keep the **PEEVED** Jews **happy** so he made <u>sure</u> Paul stayed locked up.

CHAPTER 25

LET CAESAR DECIDE...

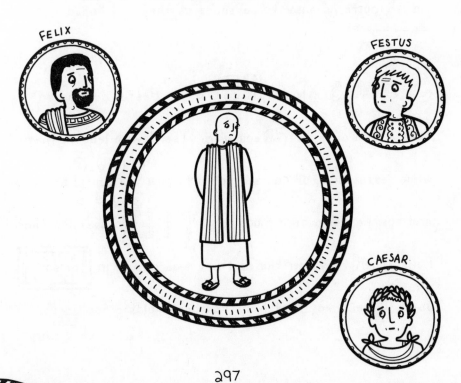

FELIX

FESTUS

CAESAR

The PEEVED Jews were quite EXCITED to hear that Festus had taken over from Felix — especially because he didn't know anything about what had happened before. They figured they might be able to persuade Festus to send Paul <back to Jerusalem so they could finally get RID of him once and for ALL. But Festus wasn't quite as easy to persuade as they had hoped.

3 days into his NEW job Festus decided to take a trip over to Jerusalem. The Jewish leaders met with Festus and, of course, told him how wonderful he was, and how he would be a much BETTER governor than Felix. Then they mentioned there was a man in prison, up in Caesarea, that Felix had been holding for ages

— they said he was very **BAD** man, and they'd *love* to take him off Festus' hands — and "take care" of him in *J*erusalem.

hmmm

The *PEEVED* Jews were still desperate to > kill < Paul, and they were hoping that if Festus would send him < back to *J*erusalem they could **sneak** up on him while he travelled. But Festus said:

"This **Paul** you're talking about — he's in *C*aesarea — right? And I'm going back there **soon**, so why don't you come back with **ME** and if he's done anything wrong we'll sort him out **THERE** and **THEN** — OK?"

So, a **week** or so **later**, Festus and the

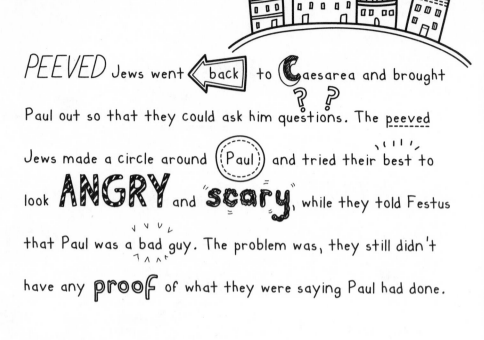

PEEVED Jews went ⟵ back ⟶ to Caesarea and brought Paul out so that they could ask him questions. The peeved Jews made a circle around (Paul) and tried their best to look ANGRY and "scary", while they told Festus that Paul was a bad guy. The problem was, they still didn't have any proof of what they were saying Paul had done.

Paul wasn't bothered AT ALL by the peeved Jews trying to "scare" him, he just STOOD there and waited until it was (his) turn to talk.

"I haven't done anything ✗ wrong. I haven't done anything ✗ wrong to the Jews, or to their TEMPLE, and I haven't done anything ✗ wrong according to the Roman **RULES**, either."

Festus looked at Paul, and then looked back at the Jews

who were chomping their teeth and growling. They looked

pretty **MAD**. Festus wanted to keep the Jews happy

— he didn't need them causing any more **trouble**, so

he said to Paul, "If I come with you ⟨back⟩ to **J**erusalem,

will you **let** me run a Roman trial for you there?"

"But **THIS IS** a Roman trial," said Paul. "I'm

already in a Roman court — you're a Roman judge!

And (you) know as well as I do that I haven't done anything

wrong. If I have done something **SO BAD** that I

deserve to **DIE** — then go ahead. But if what **these**

PEEVED Jews are saying isn't **TRUE** — you can't just let them take me away. Let Caesar decide!"

Caesar was the guy in **CHARGE** of the whole Roman Empire, and so if Paul wanted Caesar to decide — then whatever Caesar said would be **FINAL**.

Festus spoke to some of the other Roman leaders and then he announced "You want Caesar to decide? All right then, fine. Off you go."v

A few days later, before Paul had started his journey to see Caesar, Festus had some visitors.

You remember, back in chapter 12, we met KING Herod – the one who got eaten by worms? Well, his son was called Marcus Agrippa, and Agrippa and his sister were now the ones who came to visit Festus For a while. Anyway, Festus decided that Agrippa would be a GOOD person to give him some advice on what to do with Paul. So he EXPLAINED the story so far...

"OK, right, so there's this guy called Paul. Well, he used to be called Saul, but NOW he's Paul. The Jews don't like him much, and they said that when he was in Jerusalem Paul caused loads of trouble – they just seem to HATE him. Anyway, when they came here I put on a trial and told them to ACCUSE Paul of whatever it was he'd done wrong — but they just argued with him about their Jewish rules, and about this DEAD guy JESUS who Paul keeps saying is alive.

I don't really know what to do with him — I tried to send him back to Jerusalem so they could just do what they WANT with him — but he wouldn't GO. He says he wants Caesar to decide — so he's going to SEE him soon."

Agrippa listened carefully and then said he'd like to hear this guy for himself. So, Festus sent a message down to the guards and told them to bring Paul to see him in the MORNING.

All the super IMPORTANT people gathered together, and Agrippa and his sister put on their poshest clothes and lots of GOLD jewellery. (They wanted everyone to think they were AWESOME.) Then Festus TOLD the guards to bring Paul into the meeting area and said:

"KING Marcus Agrippa and all of you other important folk — look at this man. He's the ONE the Jews HATE — he's the one they want to kill. I don't think he's done anything wrong, but now he wants Caesar to decide. So I'm sending him to Rome. But I don't know what to write in my letter that will go with

him — that's **WHY** I've brought him here for you

all to see — especially **YOU** Agrippa — so that you can

all **help** me decide what I ought to say. I can't exactly

send him to Caesar without *EXPLAINING* why I'm

sending him, **CAN** I?!"

Festus smiled a **BIG** cheesy grin and looked

around at **everyone** with his thumbs up, before he

asked Paul to start talking.

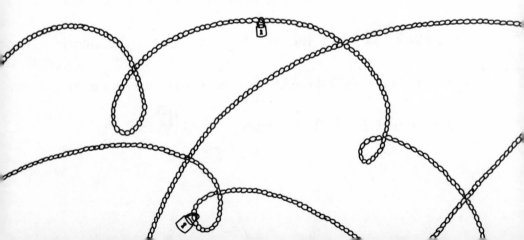

CHAPTER 26

CRAZY CHAINS...

Paul was *ABOUT* to start talking, and was rather

NOISILY clearing his throat, when **KING** Marcus

Agrippa interrupted.

Paul, I would **like** you to know that I am saying you are **ALLOWED** to speak.

Well, *THAT* was useful, thought Paul as he continued

trying to clear his throat. There must've been a bit

of fish biscuit stuck somewhere in there, achem...

achem... **FINALLY** Paul started talking:

"Thank you, King Agrippa. I'm **AMAZED** that I'm

standing here in front of you telling you about what has

happened to **ME**. I want to tell you what the Jews have said I'm like, and what they've said I've **DONE** – and **obviously**, because you know the Jewish ways so well, you'll *KNOW* what I'm on about. So, let me begin... achem... achem..."

That fish biscuit **crumb** was obviously still causing Paul a bit of *BOTHER*.

"The **Jews** know who I am, they've known me since I was knee-high to a grasshopper..." (If you think about it, grasshoppers are quite small, and if you're **ONLY** as high as a grasshopper's knee then you must be *pretty* small too – right?)

"...they've watched me grow up in **T**arsus and in **J**erusalem — I've never hidden **anything**. They can tell you that I've <u>always</u> followed all the rules — to the letter! It's **ONLY** because I have *believed* everything that God told his people hundreds and hundreds of years ago that I'm standing here now. **Everyone's** been waiting for **GOD** to send someone to save us — and he has! And it's because this has happened that **SUDDENLY** all the Jews want to kill me! Of course God can bring someone back from the **DEAD** — why is that surprising?"

The fish biscuit crumb **FINALLY** seemed to have sorted itself out — Paul was in **FULL FLOW** now!

"You ALL know that I hated Jesus *followers* — I wanted to kill them all — IN FACT I did allow quite a lot them to be **KILLED** and put a whole bunch of others into prison. I hunted them — I went round from one meeting place to another and *SNIFFED* them out. I even went to different countries to find them there!

"And when I was on a '*SNIFFING* out Jesus followers' journey **GOD** came along and smacked me in the FACE! Well, not literally — but there was a crazily **BRIGHT** **LIGHT** that blinded me for a while, and a voice that spoke in our local language and asked me **WHY** I was doing these things. It was **JESUS** himself speaking to me — and **HE** said he was going to make me someone who would tell OTHERS about him, to help people

turn back to GOD, to show people LIGHT in the

darkness and to let everyone know how much God

really loves them and wants to get to know them better."

Paul was trying to pace the floor as he was speaking,

but the chains round his ankles made it KIND OF

difficult — he so very much wanted people to

understand what had been happening.

"SO, I wasn't exactly going to ignore Jesus

speaking to me, was I? I mean, that'd be a bit stupid.

I did EXACTLY what he TOLD me to do. Everywhere

I went I TOLD people about Jesus, and I TOLD them

that God wanted them to turn back to HIM and change their lives. That's (all) I did, King Agrippa, honestly ... And now they want to KILL me. But I know that God is on my side — he's the one who's made it possible for me to be HERE standing in front of all of you. I'm only telling you that what all of GOD'S messengers have always said would happen has happened. That the one God sent to save us all would DIE and then come back to LIFE again — showing that there is real hope for everyone, no matter whether they're a Jew or a Gentile!"

Festus jumped up and started SHOUTING at Paul while tapping himself on the head and making funny faces...

Are you completely **INSANE**? Have you lost the plot? You've gone completely mad, Paul — you sound like a *crazy* man!

Everyone started to "laugh" — Festus looked **silly**, and Paul looked **CONFUSED.**

"I'm **NOT** *crazy* — I haven't lost the plot at all.

I'm telling you the truth and it all makes *SENSE*.

You've seen it all happening for yourselves, it's not like I've tried to hide **anything**. You **ALL** know what **GOD'S messengers** have said over the years — didn't you *believe* them? Did **YOU** *believe* them, King Agrippa? You *DID* — didn't you?"

"Are you *trying* to PERSUADE me to be one of your JESUS followers? You've <u>only</u> been talking for ten minutes!" said Agrippa suspiciously.

"Ten minutes or ten DAYS, I ask GOD every day that everyone who hears about JESUS will choose to follow (him.) I want YOU to be a Jesus follower, just like ME — obviously without the chains, though."

Agrippa and his sister decided it was time for a break, and got up to go outside for a while. Festus followed them, <u>trotting</u> along behind.

"So what do you **THINK**?" said Festus from behind

Agrippa's shoulder.

"He hasn't done **anything** ✗ wrong. There's nothing

we could put him in | prison | for, and certainly nothing

that means he deserves to die! If he hadn't said he wanted

to go to **Caesar** we could've just sorted it all out

here and sent him **on his way**. But now he's got

Caesar involved there's really not **MUCH** we can do."

CHAPTER 27

THE BIG BEASTY BLOWER

SO Festus and Agrippa told Paul that he'd <u>have</u> to go to **R**ome. They sent a **BIG**, **STRONG** and muscly guard called *Julius* along, too, to make sure that Paul and a bunch of other **RANDOM** prisoners didn't escape.

This was going to be our *longest* journey yet. The boat we got on was a rather <u>slow</u> one — it stopped at nearly **every** town along the way.

The first place we stopped at was called **S**idon — and we *KNEW* that Paul had some friends there who would want to **HELP** him. Muscly *Julius* was also rather a *nice* man, and he let Paul go and say (Hi) to

318

his friends — as long as he promised to come straight back.

Our journey **really** wasn't going *WELL*, the wind kept blowing us the wrong way and it was as if we were constantly fighting **AGAINST** the sea. It was *pretty* rough, and lots of people were being sick. Ewww.

EVENTUALLY, we stopped in a place called Myra and Julius decided we should try a different boat. It took **a while**, but in the end we found places on a boat that was going to Italy.

But the **NEW** boat really wasn't **much** better.

IN FACT, the weather was more of the **problem** than the boat — but either way, there was plenty more puking on this leg of the journey. We **ENDED UP** having to take a totally **RIDICULOUS** route, because every time we tried to get to land we got blown **WAY** back out again.

It seemed to be getting **WORSE** and **WORSE**, and then Paul told **everyone** that the journey was going to be <u>so</u> bad that people would **DIE** and the boat would be *RUINED*. I'm guessing he wasn't feeling <u>so</u> great — what with the stormy weather and everything — but I wasn't expecting him to be the "voice of doom"!

Julius was OBVIOUSLY feeling a bit more positive, and ignored Paul completely... AWKWARD. He decided that the captain of the boat KNEW what he was doing and agreed with him that they should just keep on going — at least to Crete. (There was a pretty decent harbour in a place called Phoenix on the island of Crete where we'd be able to tie up the boat and wait out the worst of the weather.)

But even THAT didn't quite go to plan. The strongest wind I've ever known was BLOWING and BLOWING and BLOWING, and no matter how HARD we tried we just couldn't go in the direction we wanted. All the boaty people called it the Northeaster — I think I might just call

it the BIG BEASTY BLOWER.

It was all starting to get *pretty* scary — my knees

were knocking and **everyone** looked terrified. Even

the proper boaty people, who'd done this journey LOADS

of times before, were worried. They pulled in our LITTLE

spare lifeboat that we towed along, because they wanted

to keep it SAFE. And then they did something that

got me more worried than EVER — they

actually started to tie the boat together.

They had super *long* ropes that they tied all the way

around the ship, from the top to the bottom. They **even**

dropped the anchor ⚓ — I mean, I thought that's what

you did when you wanted to **STOP** the boat, but,

apparently, it can help to **SLOW** it down and stop it

blowing over when there's a massive storm, like <u>this</u> one.

But it didn't get **any** better. We ended up having to

throw boxes of food and material and *OTHER* stuff

that we were taking to **I**taly into the sea — they were

making the boat **TOO** <u>heavy</u> and they kept flying around

all over the place and hitting people.

I **HAVE** to say, this was <u>literally</u> the **worst**

boat journey of my life. I couldn't WAIT for it to be over.

But it got even WORSE. The captain told the crew to throw everything else into the sea as well — all their boaty bits and pieces: spare ropes, buckets, scrubbing brushes, barrels of fish biscuits and anything else that wasn't fastened down.

The sky was SO dark and the sea was SO ROUGH that we couldn't even tell if it was night or day. And in the end, we gave up. We were pretty certain we were all going to die. To be honest, I was WAY past

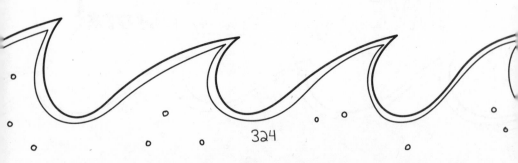

being "**scared**", I just wanted it all to stop. But

it didn't. It went on and on for **days** and **days** and

days, and all the people on the boat just sat on the

deck looking *pretty* **AWFUL**. Most of us had tied

ourselves onto something that looked **STRONG** enough

to stop us from being thrown into the sea.

And then Paul decided it was time for a LITTLE speech. It

was **HARD** to hear him over the noise of the storm

— but I think this is what he said: "I told you this wasn't

going to go **well**." Well, d'oh — I think we've *figured*

that one <u>out</u>, Paul. Can't you say something a bit more helpful?

"This wouldn't have happened if you'd *listened* to me."

ERM...no – that's **NOT** what I was hoping for.

"Be **STRONG** and **BRAVE** – you will all be OK.

The ship won't be – but **YOU** will!" That's more like it, Paul!

"God sent an  angel to speak to me last night. He

told me <u>not</u> to be afraid, and said that I will get to see

Caesar. He told me that you'd all survive this storm.

So *KEEP* going – I know God **always** keeps his

promises, he'll keep us **SAFE**. But I think we might

have to crash on an island shortly."

326

That was a *pretty good* speech, once he got going — and until he mentioned the "crash on the island" bit. But I suppose crashing on an island and being ALIVE is better than sinking on a boat and being not so alive.

Anyway. After we'd been tossed around for 2 whole WEEKS, the captain said he {thought} we might be getting near some land. So the crew kept checking how DEEP the water was and, SURE enough, it was getting shallower and shallower.

Everyone started FREAKING out and throwing all the anchors they could find off the boat so it

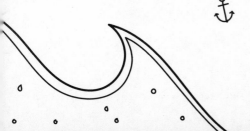

would stop before we **HIT** something — and a *FEW*

people even threw the lifeboat back into the sea. (They

told **everyone** they were just throwing over more

anchors, but *REALLY* they were trying to *figure*

out if they could use the lifeboat to escape.) Paul told Muscly

Julius and a few of the others that everyone had to

(stay) on the boat and that if anyone left God wouldn't

keep us **SAFE**. So, Julius went and found the ropes

that attached the lifeboat to the **BIG** boat and

& cut them. Then he **STOOD** there and watched the

lifeboat float away until he couldn't see it any more.

AWESOME. The people who were planning to

escape were *pretty* peeved — but there was <u>nothing</u> they

could do about it now!

Just before sunrise Paul decided it was time for some food.

We hadn't eaten for **weeks** and everyone looked

terrible. Even Muscly **Julius** wasn't looking quite so

muscly any more. I (thought) we'd thrown all the food into

the sea, but Paul seemed to produce bread from somewhere.

I don't know **WHERE** he'd got it from, but wow!

— it was **SOOOOOOO** good.

"You've all been **FREAKED** out for <u>days</u> and <u>days</u>,"

he said, "you haven't eaten anything, but you **really** need

to eat something now — or you'll starve. You will all be OK."

Then he said "thank you" to **GOD** for the bread and shared

it out. **Everyone** stared — they were so **AMAZED**

to see food that they almost didn't *DARE* to eat it. Paul took the first bite and then 'everyone' dived in — all 276 of us.

After we'd eaten we were all proper podged! We decided we wouldn't be needing any more flour to make more bread — so we *THREW* that in the sea too. Honestly, I'm SURE there couldn't possibly be anything at all left on the boat now, could there?!

EVENTUALLY, the clouds cleared a LITTLE and we could see a beach with white sand. It was quite a nice beach, really, one that would've been great for a day out if you weren't with a bunch of TOTALLY EXHAUSTED people. The captain aimed for the beach, and told **everyone** to cut the anchors loose and

put up the biggest sail ◁ so that the wind would blow us

into the sand. The captain had a *pretty good* aim and we

were doing well, but then we **SUDDENLY** came to a

crunching, cracking, creaking | stop. | We had managed to get

stuck on a big pile of sand on the bottom of the sea — and

the beach was quite a way off. Then the back of the ship

started *FALLING* apart and the sea grabbed hold of

all the pieces and took them **away**. Aaaaarrrrrgggh!

The other prisoners who had been sent with Paul looked

like they were *THINKING* of trying to escape, and

a few of the guards wanted to > kill < them. But Not-So-Muscly

-Now Julius **managed** to convince the guards that

this was stupid (idea,) and instead told **everyone** to swim for the beach in the *DISTANCE*. But not **everyone** could swim. *OOPS*.

The swimmers *WENT* for it — they used every last bit of energy they had to fight through the /waves(and get to the beach. The not-swimmers grabbed bits of boat before it all got washed away and used them like big floats. I grabbed a big *long* plank, lay down on it and used my arms and legs like big paddles — that worked *pretty* well. Maybe I should consider becoming a boat in the future...

BELIEVE it or *NOT* — everyone made it to the beach. *WOW*! Well, everyone except the boat.

CHAPTER 28

SNAKES, SICK PEOPLE & ... ROME

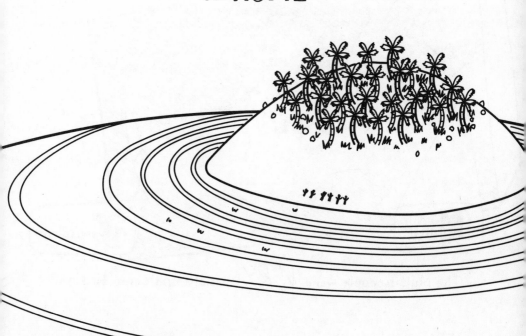

When **everyone** had managed to pick all the bits of
seaweed out of their hair and scooped all the sand out of

their **EARS**, we decided we really ought to find out where

we were. <u>I mean,</u> "white sandy beach on **RANDOM**

island near sea" isn't **much** of an address.

It turned out we were on
a *LITTLE* island called Malta.

Malta

Jerusalem

The Malta people were *VERY* friendly and came to find

us on the **BEACH**. They brought food and started a

fire for us so that we could keep warm. The weather really

hadn't improved much. It hadn't stopped raining and it

was **cold**, and I seemed to smell like a rotting fish. Bleurgh.

Hello, everyone. I'm having a ~~lovely~~ /
~~interesting~~ / ~~exciting~~ / ~~enjoyable~~ soggy
time here in Malta. Hope you are all well.
The journey was the worst ever because
I nearly (died.) The best thing about this
trip so far is Paul finding bread so we
could eat it when we were super hungry.
The weather is ~~sunny~~ / ~~warm~~ / ~~windy~~ / ~~foggy~~ /
rainy & cold. While I am here I
hope to get dry, stop smelling of fish and
stay alive. Wish you ~~were~~ / weren't here.
Lots of love from Dr Luke. x x x

Paul took on the role of becoming Mr Woodcollector — and he was actually *QUITE GOOD* at it! He came back with a great **BIG** pile of sticks to put on the fire. What he <u>hadn't</u> noticed was that there was a snake in the pile of sticks — and the snake didn't really like being put on the **FIRE**...

The snake jumped out of the fire and *BIT* Paul's hand super <u>hard</u>. So **HARD**, IN FACT , that it was just dangling there while Paul was waving his arm around. "Erm - *ouch*!" he said. "There's a snake on my hand! Help!"

But the Malta people wouldn't go **NEAR** him to help. They thought that he must be being **punished** by some random god

for doing something **evil**. But Paul shook his hand as

HARD as he could and the snake flew off and landed back

in the fire. That was the **END** of the snake.

The Malta people came a bit **CLOSER** then, and they

kept poking Paul to check if he was about to (swell) up like

a balloon or fall on the **FLOOR** dead because of

the **poison** in the snake bite — but he was totally

and completely *fine*. They were absolutely blown away

— they decided that Paul must be a god. How else could he

possibly have **survived** being bitten like that?

The **LEADER** of the Malta people was called Pub (short

for **Publius**) and he let us all go up to his **HOUSE** and stay with him for a **FEW** days. That was super kind — especially since there were still **276** of us! But Pub's dad was **really sick** and had to stay in bed.

Of course, when Paul heard about Pub's dad, he went straight $\rangle$ in and prayed for him. Then Paul put his hands on the sick man's head and he was immediately healed! Wow!

When the **REST** of the people heard what had happened they brought **ALL** the **sick** people from all over Malta and started queuing up to see Paul. Paul prayed for **every** single one of them, and all of them got **BETTER** — it was really super **AWESOME** to see all these people WELL and full of LIFE.

After a few months we were ready to carry

on our journey to Rome — and all the Malta people gave

us everything we needed to take WITH us.

I was a LITTLE bit nervous about getting on another

boat again, but this time things were a LOT easier and

the weather was pretty good. We made a few stops on

the way, as usual, and met a few Jesus followers,

too, but FINALLY we arrived in Rome.

A HUGE CROWD of people was waiting to meet

us — apparently, they'd all heard that we were coming and

had travelled from **miles** away. Seeing the **CROWDS** made Paul feel **BETTER** and **BRAVER**, and

he said "thank you" to God for sending them to meet us.

Muscly **Julius** said it was OK for Paul to find his own place in Rome, as **LONG** as there was always a soldier around to **KEEP** an eye on him. So we found a little house to live in.

A few days later, Paul went out to find the Jewish leaders. He told them his sto ry.

"I haven't done **anything** wrong, but I was captured in Jerusalem and put in prison. The Romans wanted to set me free, but the Jews wouldn't let them. That's

WHY I'm here – I've asked for Caesar to decide what happens to me. I'm NOT here to say what my people have done wrong, I'm only here to HELP you. It's because of all the WONDERFUL things that have happened, the things that can completely change your lives, that I'm here and wearing these chains."

The Jewish leaders were a LITTLE bit CONFuSEd, because they'd never even heard of Paul and no one had sent them any letters about him. Even people who'd come from Jerusalem in the LAST few months hadn't mentioned Paul, but the leaders decided they'd STILL like to hear what Paul had to say.

A few days later they all came round to

Paul's little house, and brought all of their mates with them.

People were PUSHING and SHOVING to try

and get a glimpse of Paul as he told them (all about) Jesus.

Paul talked to them for the WHOLE DAY about

everything that God had done in the PAST,

everything he'd done through JESUS and

everything he STILL wanted to do. He wanted

them to see that Jesus really was God's Son, and

he really was sent to save everyone.

"It's just like the Holy Spirit said when he spoke to God's

messenger Isaiah," said Paul. "You will hear what is said

but you won't understand it; you'll see what happens

but you just <u>won't</u> get it. Everyone's heart isn't

open to GOD any more, they hardly hear what he says

and it's like they have their eyes SHUT when he does

AMAZING things. If they had open ears and open

eyes, they'd see just how wonderful he is and then they'd

turn back to him and he would <u>heal</u> them."

(Isaiah? (say Eyes-eye-er) Isaiah was one of God's

messengers hundreds and hundreds of years before Jesus

came to earth. Isaiah told people that GOD was going

to send someone to save them — and that someone was

Jesus! You can find out lots more about all the things

Isaiah said if you have a Bible. It's all written

down in a book called "<u>Isaiah</u>"!)

The crowds started to **wander** off. Some of them

believed him, but some of them didn't, and they kept arguing

with each other about who was right and who was wrong.

"I want you to know that this is all **TRUE**!" shouted

Paul as they all walked **AWAY**. "God sent Jesus

for **ALL** of us, the Jews and the Gentiles — and the

Gentiles are *listening*!"

Paul stayed in his LITTLE HOUSE for 2 whole years and

loads of people came to visit him. As always, he kept on

telling people about **JESUS** — no matter what.

He was **STRONG** and **BRAVE** and he was determined

that nothing was going to stop him telling the whole world!

345

I **suppose** you might be wondering if Paul ever *DID*

get to see Caesar and what actually happened to him...

Well, firstly, he **kept on** talking about JESUS.

Secondly, he saw a Caesar called **Nero**, who set him free.

Thirdly, he travelled around all over the place to keep on

TELLING people about Jesus and he wrote loads

and loads of letters. Good old Paul.

(If you have a **Bible** you can read about everything

that happened to Paul and some of the letters that he

wrote — you'll find them listed as "Romans",

"Corinthians", "Galatians", "Ephesians",

"Philippians", "Colossians", "Thessalonians" and

"Philemon" — to name but a few. ENJOY!)

DID YOU KNOW that Christians *believe* Peter and Paul's story is far **more** than just that... They believe it's all **100%** true. You can read their story for yourself in a **Bible**, you'll find it listed as "Acts" or maybe "The Acts of the Apostles".

If you'd like to find out **more** about what Christians believe then visit (www.scriptureunion.org.uk) or ask at your local **CHURCH**.

Keep on the lookout for the **NEXT** instalment of 'Diary of a Disciple' – it won't be *long*!

www.diaryofadisciple.org